Written With Rhyme and Reason

Catching the Current in Events

Annette Adams

Written With Rhyme and Reason
by Annette Adams

Printed in the United States of America

ISBN 1-594670-69-2

Xulon Press
www.XulonPress.com

Xulon Press books are available in bookstores everywhere,
and on the Web at www.XulonPress.com.

I dedicate this book
to my greatest encourager,
my husband, Lane Adams.

Acknowledgements

My other great encouragers for the production of this volume are a host of friends to whom I have been mailing out individual poems for about the last ten years. As time went by, some of them said they had no more room on their refrigerators to post the poems and that I ought to put them all together in a book. (These poems were usually sent either to catch the current in events or in observance of some holiday).

On a personal level, I would like to acknowledge the help of my daughter, Susie Moore and my granddaughter, Ashley Moore, who patiently cleaned up the grammar and punctuation. I would also like to express my appreciation to my son-in-love, T M. Moore, for preparing the final manuscript on disk, and my granddaughter, Kristy Bobb, whose enthusiasm spurred me on.

After the publication of my book "The Desert Rat", a biography concerning the remarkable life of Aileen Coleman, letters of appreciation for it often ended by saying: "But when will we see your book of poetry?" Well, dear friends, here it is!

Foreword

I asked my son-in-law. T. M. Moore, to write my Foreword for me, which he chose to do in poetry form. You will find this on the following page.

He has had two books of poetry published: "Celtic Flame" and "Ecclesiastes: Ancient Wisdom When All Else Fails." His incidental poems have been printed in over thirteen different publications.

THE BALLAD TAMER

2 Corinthians 10:3-5

For Mom

"Lay hold on every thought and make
it serve the Lord above;
Subdue it, subjugate it, take
It captive to His love."

She fixes her deep-seeing eye
On common things and great,
And loads each verse her hand may try
With glory's heavy weight.

One form above all others rules
My mother's lyric art;
Exquisite skills and well-honed tools
Obey her mind and heart.

This ancient form so often used
For trivial songs and rhymes
Is with skeltonic lyric fused
To draw out things sublime.

What pleasure must our Lord derive
From her uncommon skill,
Who tames this form and always strives
To make it serve God's will.

What joy as well do we indulge
To read her artistry
And find therein God's love divulged
Afresh, for all to see.

Write on then, Ballad Tamer! May
Fresh visions fill your heart;
And may the Lord have His own way
In all your much-loved art.

Love,
Your T.

Introduction

"He did it without rhyme or reason" is an old saying we've heard many times in the past. When considering a title for my collection of writings, I realized that I had written poetry *with* rhyme and reason. Thus, my title and the layout for the book; the reason will appear on the left and the rhyme will appear on the right.

I've been reminded of the fact that "this just isn't done". But, as my daughter, Susie said: "Just because it isn't done doesn't mean that it couldn't or shouldn't be done. For instance, think of the Art world. Doesn't it enhance Wyeth's painting, 'Christina's World', to know the story behind it?"

I have sought to "catch the current in events" in the world and our everyday life. I have tackled everything from politics to puppy dogs.

I invite you to consider, then lament, laugh or praise God with me.

Table of Contents

I.
The Current In Events ***19***

"Voices" *21*
"A Time of Terror" *23*
"Politricks" *25*
"Lost and Found" *27*
"Abortion" *31*
"Throw Aways" *35*
"From One Hypocrite To Another" *37*
"Put on" By Mother Nature *39*
"What If?" *41*
"Jesus Is The Answer" *45*
"Idol Worship" *49*
"Myopic Morality" *53*

II.
Poems For Special Days ***55***

"Memorial Day" *57*
"What's Good?" *61*
"Christmas Gift" *65*
"Easter" *67*
"Trite Tidings" *69*
"Love Letters" *73*
"The Empty Tomb" *77*
"Christmas Bestivities" *79*
"Jesus (*No Longer a Baby)"* *81*
"Christmas Feast" *83*
"Where is Peace?" *85*

III.
Behind The "Seens" ***87***

"Flamentations" *89*
"I Wonder As I Wander" *91*
"Picture Me" *93*
"You Can Begin Anew" *97*
"Call It What You Will" *99*
"Why Me?" *101*
"What Kind Of Man Is This?" *103*
"I Thought You'd Call Me Father" *105*

IV.
A Bit Of Wit ***107***

"Directional Dyslexia" *109*
"Dental Definitions" *111*
"A Slip of the Lip" *113*
"Those Moldin' Golden Years" *115*
"Bone(a) Fid(o) Beauty" *119*
"The Meter Maid" *123*
"Written With *Rim* and Reason" *125*
"A *Trill*-ogy" *127*

V.
Eternal Expectations ***129***

"Morning Glory" *131*
"Locked Out" *135*
"Remember Me" *137*
"The Full Cup" *139*
"Forever Me" *141*
"Bough in Worship" *145*

VI.
When Friends Come To Mind ***147***

"The Grandfather Clock" *149*
"When Alice Comes To Mind" *151*
"The Desert Rat" *155*
"A Rose" *157*
"Duff" *159*
"Matthew" *161*
"Long Distance Love" *163*

VII.
All In The Family ***165***

"A Mother's Memories" *167*
"It Isn't That You Do Not Care" *171*
"Mother To Mother" *175*
"The Home-acher" *177*
"Clean" *179*
"Age 13" *181*
"The Sewing Kit" *183*
"My Room" *185*
"When Stars Fall From Our Eyes" *187*
"To Ashley—With love, from God" *189*
"Look Ahead" *191*
"Maybe" *193*
"Moving Words" *195*
"I Forget" *197*

I.

CATCHING THE CURRENT IN EVENTS

The world says: "There is no absolute truth".

Jesus Christ says: "I AM the truth. Everyone on the side of truth listens to Me."
(John 14:6 and 18:37b)

Voices

Voices, voices,
The world's and His,
Choices, choices,
That's all there is.

If I wrote everyday, for the rest of my life, I could not possibly express with words the emotions I experienced on September 11, 2001.As a young girl, I remember hearing the words, from the mouth of Franklin D. Roosevelt, after Pearl Harbor was attacked: "December 7, 1941 is a day that will live in infamy". Many horrible years of war followed that devastating day. I could not believe that I had lived long enough to hear similar words again…and, this time, with little or no prospect of an end to war.

The impact of the Tower Terror was too much to assimilate at once. (One will probably never be able to take it all in—ever). But, as I began to work through my own feelings of shock, pain, fears and grief; and as I struggled to crawl out from under all of this emotional wreckage, I finally found the strength to ask, weakly: "what's to be learned from all this—for me—the only person I have any control over at all"? I was gently guided back to the same "Free"Way, with the same directions and warning signs that have always been there—The Word of God: (II Chronicles 7:14) "If MY people, which are called by My Name, shall humble themselves and pray, and turn from their wicked ways; then will I hear from heaven and forgive their sin, and will heal their land". As a wise friend, Mrs. Pat Hunter, once said to me (concerning a personal problem): "You've paid a high price for this lesson, Annette—don't miss it".

Writing this poem was a helpful step in my own healing process.

A TIME OF TERROR

(September 11, 2001)

A time to live—a time to die,
A time when horror hit the sky.
All eyes were stunned by flames and crashes,
Buildings weeping tears of ashes.

A time to scream—a time to pray,
As darkness drenches night and day.
The smell of hell with no relief,
The hoping, groping gut-filled grief.

It mattered not what age or race,
But only: "Have you seen this face?"
A time to search, below, above,
The sight of fright, the look of love.

We've seen the worst that man can do
To men they never even knew.
But oh the many heroes found,
Those 'folks of steel' on Zero Ground.

I do not want to miss Your voice,
I know the fears in "freedom's choice."
Just help ***me*** Lord, free ***me*** from sin,
And cleanse my lens to see within.

A time to dig through hate and rages,
'Time to seek our "Rock of Ages",
Grieving over man-made-crime,
Our God, Who 'Towers" over time.

I am aware of the fact that Politics has long been known to have a bed partner called corruption, but felt that our country had reached a new level of low, morally speaking, under the leadership of Bill Clinton. As we were daily dragged through degrading dirty-linen-discussions of what sex "is or isn't," my "sense had been seared beyond sensibility."

My feelings ran the gamut from shock to embarrassment, both in the way the leader of the supposedly greatest country in the world was comporting himself, and the media's (and public's) often unbelievably insipid reaction to him.

I finally exploded in the form of poetry. Thus, "Politricks" erupted.

"POLITRICKS"

They're playing a game, what political shame,
Using words to confuse and to label.
The truth's seldom heard. It is slurred, often blurred,
It's like facing a new "Tower of Babel".

Remember the fun when the old quartets sung
In that barbershop harmony way?
"Oh, where is the **sin** in **sin**cere?" they'd moan,
Or "the **good** in **good**bye?" they'd say.

Well, now speakers hamper, oh my how they tamper
With promises, words said in vain.
They resonate right and our hopes they excite,
But they end up like "clouds without rain."

Our polls make no sense, there is just no defense,
"You can sin and still win", they have said.
But why can't we buy that a lie is a lie
Whether said in or out of the bed?

Our country, of course, has the cart 'fore the horse;
We have all been completely outwitted:
We are asked to embrace, overlook and show grace.
To forgive something *never admitted.*

Yes, forgiveness we know is the right thing to show,
But we've missed, so resist, one great fact:
First, see your condition that calls for contrition,
Confess it, then "clean up your act."

No one will debate "Family Values" sounds great,'
But that term they affirm has its flaws.
'Cause its meaning for me might be different from thee,
For that script may be stripped of God's Laws.

So let's face the fact, it's a standard we've lacked,
We are fools without rules in this land.
And those sick "Politricks" we will not ever fix
Till on **His Ten Commands** we all stand.

It began to dawn on me, somewhat suddenly, that so many words that had once been an important part of my vocabulary—and the forming of my character—were seldom, if ever, being used anymore. I missed them—deep in my innermost being.

It saddens me to see what is happening to our society as "the world" has been slowly stripping away God's moral standards—the Ten Commandments. (It's like the old saying: "If you throw a frog into a pot of boiling water, he'll immediately jump out, but if you put him in cold water and slowly bring it to a boil, he'll get caught and die there"). This attempt to eradicate God from the very minds of the people—and then never seem to connect this fact to what is causing all the serious problems—the killings, drugs, cheating, lying, greed, ad nauseam—is staggering. It's a burgeoning blindness that is bound to result in chaos, crime and misery of all kinds. When someone says "I think this is right, or I think this is wrong", no one bothers to ask the question: "According to whose standards"? I truly miss the quality of life we once knew, here in America. Thus, the reason for this poem.

(This poem was published in the "Values Realization Institute" Journal of 1997)

LOST AND FOUND

I'm in search of something missing,
It's been lost; it's very scary.
I'm afraid I can't replace it,
It's my old vocabulary.

"Confession" and "contrition", words
We often used to hear,
Like "repentance", "sin", and "holiness"
Have seemed to disappear.

The words that gave life purpose,
All God's stabilizing truth,
Which defined our country's calling
Are now hidden from our youth.

The rules we used to count on
To restrain our nation's flaws,
Have been changed, all rearranged,
Protecting those who break the laws.

Try to quote the Ten Commandments,
You'll be stopped, or laughed to scorn.
'No matter that we're robbed and raped
And children die—unborn.

"Accountability" is gone,
We're left with its debris;
Just "put the blame on Mame", or
Almost anyone but me.

"Judge not that ye be not judged"
Is now a phrase that's really "in."
Is this attitude of latitude
To justify *our* sin?

Which, hence, presents a problem,
Making choices as we should:
Just whose standard are we using
As we're choosing bad from good?

And "tolerance", that worn out word
Is emphasized each day.
It covers every life style known,
Except the Christian Way.

All the world is re-defining, undermining
Words we knew
As they're emptied of their meaning,
Sadly, lives are emptied, too.

But, I've found this truth is sound:
His Words will never ever vary.
Though we lose, abuse, misuse them,
They remain **"God's Dictionary."**

This must be the saddest reigning result of ignoring God's laws that exists today. But as I thought of all the babies being killed in their mother's womb, I must admit I also felt some anger about the "double standard" that has been present in our society as long as I can remember. Young men seemed almost encouraged to "sow some wild oats" while they were young, and the girls who participated in this immoral activity were often left "holding the bag", so to speak, simply because of the bodily differences in men and women. (I realize that these days of "free (?) sex" make it even easier for the woman to get pregnant).

I can appreciate the sincere motivation of the marchers against abortion. But I personally feel they're "striking out" because they've missed first base. I believe they're starting in the middle of the chapter. Wouldn't it be far more to the point to march against fornication and adultery—the real father of the crime? (Lotsa luck getting up a load for that march!)

God's Standard is not a double one. It calls both men and women into accountability for their moral behavior. God's way provides a safe womb for all babies and a secure home for all mothers.

I love what Jude 21a (Living Bible translation) says: "Stay always within the boundaries where God's love can reach and bless you".

I wrote this poem with a heavy heart.

ABORTION

America, this place most blessed
Is finally falling, like the rest.
We've brought it on by our own hand,
This blight, that's come across our land.

We're left in shock, we point the blame,
And miss the means through which it came.
We've heard "safe sex" proclaimed so long;
But contraception won't right wrong.

So where does all this crime begin?
With good ol' "number seven sin".
As we examine God's ten laws,
Adultery is the basic cause.

Results are found in woman's womb,
To bring forth life or cause its doom.
But there's no choice, for God has said:
"I make you live or make you dead".

We wonder, when does life begin?
And blind ourselves to what's within.
If "*this*" weren't "*live*", why does "*it*" grow?
Why get "*it*" out? I want to know.

But, men, if you "pick up that stone"
Remember this, and this alone:
From that decision you are free,
For pregnant you will never be.

So, I hope males who demonstrate
Will ask: "Did I participate?
Could I have ever caused this grief
And just walked out, with great relief?"

We follow blindly all we see
In movies, magazines, TV,
'Til lives are left with dirty dregs,
And no way to unscramble eggs.

2.

We're daily dosed with dressed-up-lies,
That just confuse or tantalize:
"Sure, wear that bathing suit so sheer,
But don't go near the water, dear."

The world is teasing, tempting all;
To satisfy our lusts, we fall.
With standards gone, we've no defense,
So they exploit our decadence.

And, what's that "innocent act", I cry,
"That will not hurt the other guy?"
With misused freedom, we can't win,
We end up, sadly, slaves to sin.

Just as King David wrecked his life
By sleeping with Uriah's wife,
He next planned death—to cover fright,
But learned "two wrongs don't make a right."

'Same sequence is in play today:
We cover sin this heinous way,
And seem to be so slow to know
"We always reap just what we sow."

This fearful freedom plagues us still,
To keep His laws or our own will.
But we each find, ironically,
I don't break them, but they break me!

Our God demands we change our course
And halt this murder at its source.
If "statute Seven" we would heed,
Abortions we would seldom need.

I've been so grieved by all the insecurities expressed by people I've talked to these days. Women are longing for "A Sunday Kind Of Love, a love that lasts past Saturday night" (as sung by Fran Warren with the Claude Thornhill orchestra, during the Big Band era). Our children are in need of "someone to come home to" and to guide them, morally, spiritually and every other way. Men need to know they, too, are loved, that they can also trust their contracts and the word of other men. Both kids and adults are being given 'things' as a substitute for time and love.

Most of our merchandise is made to last but a temporary time—hardly worth taking home, etc…etc. Few products and few people are "built for the long haul", today. It is disconcerting to say the least; so little seems to last. It's truly a temporary-tinsel-time.

This was written to pour a little balm on this sad situation.

Throw Aways

We live in a time of throw aways, of go aways, today.
Most vows that have been spoken have been broken, gone astray.
Where nothing merits mending, only ending—why begin?
Whether toy, or girl or boy, let's just destroy—or turn it in.

When even a sweet baby is a "maybe" in the womb,
His helpless voice will have no choice; his mother seals his doom.
Today's the day to play around, let sex abound—deceiving.
If babies come, Dad's on the run, the fun is done—he's leaving.

One seldom hears: "Let's save it or engrave it; it's worthwhile".
Things fall apart, won't even start, or just go out of style.
Most goods become erasable, replaceable, so fast;
No permanence, short-termanence; is nothing made to last?

But, Someone's into caring and repairing me and you;
He takes the time to clean our grime, then saves and makes us new.
God's Son is into reaping, mending, keeping all that be,
And He won't ever throw away or go away from me.

I have a good friend, who loves the Lord with his whole heart, and sometimes longs to share Jesus with his fellow workers—whom he also loves. He was feeling so discouraged one day, because he said that often when he tried to share, the men would respond: "There are just too many hypocrites in the Church." (I was tempted to suggest that he say: "Granted, and we have room for one more.")

He then asked if I could possibly write something helpful on the subject. This poem was an effort to do just that.

FROM ONE HYPOCRITE TO ANOTHER

Most folks have heard the comment:
"All those hypocrites in the Church...".
Well, amused by this deception
I began my own research.

First, we must define the word,
Which Webster makes so clear:
It's "one who acts like what he ain't".
That hits us all, I fear.

The people picking on this group
That seeks to find the cure,
Have best described themselves, me thinks,
"The hypocrites", for sure.

'Cause when they see a mirror,
And look at their own face,
They'd better ask this question:
"Am I covered by His grace?"

For when we join the Church of God
We sinners must admit:
That "only Jesus' precious blood
Can heal this hypocrite."

Psalm 19:1-3 says:
"The heavens declare the glory of God,
The skies proclaim the work of His Hands,
Day after day they pour forth speech;
Night after night they display knowledge.
There is no speech or language
Where their voice is not heard."

When I heard the TV announcer say: "Be on the lookout for a great spectacular put on by Mother Nature, tonight," it penetrated my thinking in a brand new way. *"Put on by Mother Nature????"* Hold on! This was just another illustration of the frog boiling away in the pot—just another example of an attempt, albeit seemingly innocent, to remove God from the very minds of the people.

Ole Santa has taken over at Christmastime; the bunnies, baskets, and eggs monopolize Easter; and The Creator is now being called Mother Nature.

This poem, "PUT ON" BY MOTHER NATURE is an effort on my part to expose that vacuous vocabulary which has put quite a few unaware generations into that pot; and we are slowly "boiling away."

"Put On" By Mother Nature

The TV news blared forth its views
"There'll be the greatest show
Put on by 'Mother Nature',
All the sky will be aglow.

With meteors and shooting stars,
All shining bright tonight,
You'll see this great phenomenon,
This flare, this rare delight".

But what caught my attention
Was just who would be my host:
"Put on by Mother Nature"
Must surprise our God the most.

The Word says "He was in the world",
His treatment here was grim.
The world still won't acknowledge
That "All things were made by Him".

"Ms Nature" gets the credit
For those great displays of glory,
But all "natural disasters"
Call for quite another story.

Insurers charge a premium—
I find this rather odd—
To cover earthquakes, storms and floods,
All labeled "Acts of God".

How long can we evade
That God has made all things that be,
And all because he loves the world.
Is this so hard to see?

"The Greatest Show On Earth"
Our God produces day and night.
And it wasn't "Mother Nature"
Who first said: "Let there be light"!

I was meditating on the amazing love of God, one day, and reviewing one of my favorite Old Testament verses: Deuteronomy 5:29…the Lord is speaking to Moses…"Oh, that there were such an heart in them that they would fear Me and keep all my Commandments always so that it would go well with them and their children forever". I was stunned by the fact that I'd always just taken for granted that my God was a God of love. "What if" He weren't? (Many others have worshipped cruel gods). So I pondered how He might respond to our cries for help, and how He might guide us, if He answered us like "the world" does— rather than with His Words of Truth. How devastating! How futile! How hopeless! Thus, "What If?" pushed its way through my pen.

WHAT IF?

What if there were no God of love,
But just a God of hate?
What if He didn't care at all
About our future state?

What if He had not given rules
To show us wrong from right?
Let's see how He would help us
Were He darkness 'stead of light?

"Oh Lord, my husband's left me,
And he's broken every vow!"
"WHY NOT? SHE'S SO MUCH YOUNGER ~~
SO MUCH PRETTIER THAN THOU!"

"She lied to me; I trusted her.
It pierced me like a knife.
Oh God, please help ~~please answer."
"I GUESS, MY DEAR, THAT'S LIFE!"

"They stole our lifetime savings, Lord;
Those mean 'Uriah Heepers'.
Please help us get our money back."
"TOUGH LUCK! IT'S FINDERS KEEPERS

"A drunken driver hit our child;
She'll never be the same."
"WELL, HE IS NOT RESPONSIBLE ~~
THE ALCOHOL'S TO BLAME!"

"TV provides much pleasure, but
There's so much sex and crime."
"WATCH OFTEN ~~ MORALS SOFTEN;
YOU'LL GET USED TO IT IN TIME."

"Our marriage is in trouble, God;
Your guidance is a must."
"OMIT 'COMMIT', AND 'HOLY WRIT',
FOR LOVE IS MOSTLY LUST!"

"And what about abortion, Lord;
Since when is murder kind?"
IT ALL DEPENDS ON THIS YEAR'S TRENDS.
I JUST MIGHT CHANGE MY MIND!"

"We've 'had it' with our children ,
With the troubles that they bring."
"WELL, LET THEM GO ~~THEY'LL SOMEHOW GROW ~~
YOU NEED TO DO YOUR THING!"

"That man committed incest;
Stop him now ~~ don't let him go!"
"AH, JUST COMMEND HIS COURAGE
FOR APPEARING ON THAT SHOW!"

"He stole a gun and killed my son.
You must condemn at last!"
"WHAT ROT!! HE'S NOT ACCOUNTABLE;
HE'S HAD A TROUBLED PAST!

"We're not allowed to judge, today;
Discernment seems the sin."
"DON'T BE ABSURD; THE RULES ARE BLURRED,
AND 'TOLERANCE' IS 'IN'!"

"We all knew he was guilty, but
He won the case with ease."
"YOU KNOW THERE ARE NO LONGER RULES,
BUT ONLY REFEREES!"

"Oh God, I've hurt my dearest friend:
My tongue its venom spat!
But I know you'll forgive me.."
"YEH, WHOEVER TOLD YOU THAT??"

"Our leaders break their promises;
You must observe our plight."
"MY CHILD, YOU WILL DISCOVER SOON
THAT LYING IS ALL RIGHT!!"

"Now, Christians live just like the world,
You surely, God, must rue it!"
"YOU THOUGHT WHEN I INSPIRED THIS WORD,
I MEANT FOR YOU TO DO IT??"

What if there were no justice?
No Godly-guiding Hands?
No merciful perspective?
No clear-cut Ten Commands?

It's plain to see how sad "twould be
Were we to be resigned
To 'bad is good' and 'good is bad' ~~
Behaviors undefined.

Christ kept that law ~~ without a flaw,
And then, for us, He died.
What if when we'd believed, received,
God simply said, "I LIED!!??"

'What if' is pure conjecture,
But surely we can see
Humanity's insanity's
Aren't God's morality.

His Character's consistent.
His love won't lead astray.
His answers come in black and white.
NO "IFS", NO "BUTS", NO GRAY!

We are all besieged by bumper sticker brazenness every time we ride the roadways. The messages range anywhere from cute to crass—from humorous to degrading. But the ones "advertising" Jesus cause more than a little discomfort in me (particularly when the car sporting the message rudely moves in front of me).

A person must be seeking Jesus sincerely and asking the right questions in order to get satisfying answers from Him. (And I **do** believe that we must always be ready to give an answer to "*those who ask a reason for the hope that is within us").* Yes, I **do** believe "Jesus **is** the answer", but giving His Name a ride through town on a bumper sticker doesn't quite "get it" for me.

This poem is written in a serio-comedy format, depicting a cynical search for truth and showing the futility of giving answers to questions that aren't being asked.

JESUS IS THE ANSWER

So, "Jesus is the answer"
All those bumper stickers blaze;
Put some feet on—get some meat on
That ol' churned out, burned out phrase.

"I have heard that God is everywhere,
This 'Heaven-Hunting-Hound;
Why is it He won't visit me?
He never hangs around."

"I've studied world philosophies,
I've even read God's Book:
'Saw lots of 'nots', 'begets', 'begots',
Not worth a second look."

"I pray when I'm in trouble,
And I'm sure His hearing's fine.
But when I call, I get the stall,
There's no one on the line".

"There's such a bad connection
'Tween this Jesus Man and me,
He does not fit from where I sit;
Explain this mystery."

Well, Jesus is the answer,
But to fully "see the Light",
It's like playing that game, Jeopardy,
Your question must be right.

If you're asking: "Who created me,
The world, the stars, the sun?"
Then, Jesus is the answer,
For our God and He are One.

2.

If you ask, sincerely, "How can I,
A sinner, see your face?"
You'll hear His loving answer:
"'Cause I died and took your place."

If you ask "What then will please You,
End the rift and lift the shade?"
He will answer: "Trust, obey My Word,
My Spirit will invade."

Yes, Jesus is The Answer
To repair your dabbling doubt;
But first, believe, receive Him,
Then He'll clear your hearing out.

So, when you see that trite—
That bumper byte banality,
Think through all this inane
"one size fits all" mentality.

He'll surely cure that vision blur
And give us perfect sight;
Yes, "Jesus IS the answer",
But your questions must be right.

Jeremiah 10:5 (New International Version) states: "Like a scarecrow in a melon patch, their idols cannot speak; they must be carried because they cannot walk. Do not fear them; they can do no harm, nor can they do any good".

We are so guilty of worshipping idols, in America. But because they're not forged in gold and shaped like a calf, we're dangerously oblivious to it. We are warned that trusting in anything or anyone—other than God—is futile. It's His very first commandment: "You shall have no other Gods before Me". (Exodus 20:3)

My poem, "Idol Worship" seeks to bring this truth home to our own back yard.

Idol Worship

As Jeremiah warned us, in
His message, so unique:
"Like a scarecrow in a melon patch"
Their idols cannot speak."

Today, we fashion gods of gold,
Of beauty and of power,
of intellect, unearned respect,
Which all, in time, turn sour.

Our busy phones call ol' Dow Jones,
He'll show our bankrolls full.
But they can often get quite "bear",
When he's run out of "bull".

So. if our idol's money,
Worldly wealth one of our goals,
We're apt to find that cash we stash
In "bags just full of holes".

Perhaps we worship beauty;
Who cares if you're not rich?
But that, too, fades when age pervades,
So that won't "scratch our itch".

Let's make "the mind" our idol.
Higher learning must be good.
But, trust in man? You never can!
He might as well be wood.

Education without morals,
We have seen, is quite insane.
For he who steals from boxcars,
When taught well, can steal the train.

2.

And many worship power,
Making others "toe the line".
But they'll soon know, for God will show
"All power on earth is mine".

As Jeremiah warned us,
Our dead idols cannot speak.
"Like scarecrows in a melon patch"
Our prayers are "up the creek"

As I awaken each morning, only to see our world becoming more chaotic, I am both saddened and frightened. What has become of our precious freedom? It would appear that our freedom has slowly degenerated into but a license to sin: freedom **from** fidelity, freedom **from** accountability of any kind, while daily fighting for more freedom **from** God. The most shocking blindness to me is that very few seem to note the correlation between trying to remove God from the very minds of the people (anything that smacks of religion is becoming illegal) and the utter chaos which has followed. It's often no longer safe to go to school or walk out your front door. Without self government no democracy will work.

We have our service men spread out all over the world supposedly trying to protect others and to promote our way of life—one that isn't working for us anymore. When is America going to wake up and see that without God's standard for right and wrong—the Ten Commandments—we will only continue to have more chaos each day? Only the One who made this world can know and show us how to best survive in it.

"The god of this age has blinded the minds of unbelievers so that they cannot see the light of the Gospel of the glory of Christ, who is the Image of God. (II Corinthians 4:4).

This distorted vision—this blanket of blindness—that covers the mind and the heart is what prompted me to write MYOPIC MORALITY.

Myopic Morality

"Remove those Ten Commandments,
I don't want them on the wall.
I won't have them in the school room,
Those restrictions I appall!

For what I want is freedom,
My own Edom—my own choice.
My own opinion runs my life,
I listen to my voice.

'Don't care a whit for fairness,
Or for "careness" of another.
My love for me goes deeper,
I'm no "keeper of my brother".

How dare God try to hamper,
Put a damper on my fun.
I'll act the fool—break every rule
Before my life is done.

But I'm against those 'hate crimes',
(Which must cause our God above
To ask this clear-cut question:
"Just what crime is done through love?")

I often want what others have,
My lusts I won't deny.
So why not murder, fornicate,
And covet, steal or lie?"

This brings to a conclusion
This confusion everywhere;
A lot of feet are stuck in muck—
Are planted in mid-air.

And this myopic vision blinds
What obviously is true:
Without God's laws that other guy
Can "do it unto you".

II.

POEMS FOR SPECIAL DAYS

Like all of us, I had carried around painful memories, from the past, that I had managed to blissfully bury for quite a few years. But I felt that the time had come for me to unbind the thoughts and free them at last!

It was in the 40's—World War II days. I was chosen sponsor of our Joliet Township High School 500 member, all boy, National Championship Band. It was a great honor. I was looking forward to the promised prize of accompanying the band to California. But the attack on Pearl Harbor changed everything. Our "prize" turned out to be the opportunity to go down to the train station a couple of times a week and play music while all the boys left for war. We did that for our whole senior year, as they left and left and left. Yes, it WAS a privilege, but so soaked with sadness that it was indescribable.

A couple of years later, in the midst of my College years, I began dancing professionally (having studied all forms of dance from age 6 on). I began in the Empire Room of the Palmer House Hotel, in Chicago. During that time, besides performing and attending school, we often did Benefits at the Veterans Hospitals in the Chicago area. One particular occasion supplied another reason for writing this poem. We were performing on a round stage that was surrounded by two rows of what they called "basket cases"—men with no arms or legs. After my eyes were able to focus on this audience, my body continued to perform what it was trained to do, but only through almost paralyzing shock. After the performance was over we were taken on a "tour" of the hospital wards. I wanted to blot sight of all this sorrow out of my mind forever— I didn't want to remember any of it. But I wrote this poem because I must always remember—we ALL MUST!

MEMORIAL DAY

I was there when all those 'boys' my age,
Went off to fight a war,
And I was there when those same 'men'
Returned to us no more.

I've entertained those heroes
On their barren beds of pain,
Those glory-gutted veterans
Who, to this day, remain.

Have you ever been in a holding pen
Where we keep those 'dregs of war'?
Behind sad eyes, you hear their cries:
"Was this worth fighting for?"

I've seen those haunting grave yards,
Causing tears to blur my sight,
Those endless rows of crosses
Making fields of silent white.

Their voices plead: "Remember me,
I heard my country's call,
I, too, was free to hide or flee,
Instead, I gave my all."

But while we are remembering those
Who 'died to make men free...'
And thinking of those crosses,
Signs of death for liberty;

Let's not forget the One who
When He heard His Father's call,
Who, too, was free to hide or flee,
But chose to give His all.

He faced a world at war with sin,
No friends marched by His side,
No flags waved in His honor,
All alone, for us, He died.

But that grave could not keep Him.
Nor forever still His breath.
He won that 'war-to-end-all-wars',
Demolished demon-death.

So, remember those white crosses
And those sacrifices grim,
But remember, too, the cross of Christ,
There's hope because of Him.

"All hail the power of Jesus' Name..."
We still can sing His praise,
Because His cross cures death's dark loss
And brings eternal days.

This is dealing with our "Happy **Hollow**days" that have become so entrenched in empty rituals and confused theology. We seem to be in danger of missing the very heart of Christmas.

WHAT'S GOOD?

What's good about a holiday
That most have come to dread,
Because it seldom opens hearts,
But pocketbooks instead?

What's good about those Carols
Ringing out from store to store,
When no one hears those lovely words
Or heeds them anymore?

What's good about a "Baby's" life
That sorrow occupied?
What's good about "Good Friday"
If all ended when He died?

What's good about the "Good Book"
If you never look inside?
What's good about "Good News"
If it's not true or even tried?

What's good about our Jesus?
He's called good, that's not denied.
But He said, "I'm the Son of God".
He's not good if He lied.

What's good about the Gospel:
"Saved by faith", to justify,
If we must still earn heaven
Why did Christ, for God's sake, die?

Why celebrate this birth, if life on earth
Was all He had?
It's His great resurrection
That makes all those "tidings glad."

We need His whole "sweet story";
That must be understood,
For Christmas without Easter
Isn't merry—even good.

Yes, we can wish good tidings,
Hallelujah, peace, good cheer
Because that Living Son of God
Still rules; He reigns; He's here!

One day I was completely overwhelmed by the absolutely thrilling theology involved in God's mysterious and merciful plan to redeem all who might believe in His Son, Jesus.

His patience and love continue to steadily drip from this cup of kindness called Salvation! *(II Peter 3:9 "The Lord is not slow in keeping His promise, as some understand slowness. He is patient with you, not wanting anyone to perish, but everyone to come to repentance").*

I longed to express my awe and gratitude.

(This was the very first Christmas poem I ever wrote and was put on the front of the Christmas Edition of the Presbyterian Journal, in 1981. Reverend Aiken Taylor was the editor, at that time, and Joel Belz was the managing editor).

CHRISTMAS GIFT

Jesus...born, torn, crucified;
My "gift" upon the tree.
Died, alive, satisfied
The will of God for me.

I, pride aside, justified,
Will one day see His face;
Because of love personified...
God's present, wrapped in grace.

This is the "Main event"! Easter is what validates all other Christian Celebrations. This is what puts Christ above all others. This is why we follow Him. **He is alive**. The high price paid by God—in Christ— to redeem man is only overshadowed by the inexpressible love that authored it. Words don't exist to praise Him properly. I tried.

("Because I live, you shall live also" John 14:19)

Easter

In His love again immersed,
The painful pageant is rehearsed.
'Crucifixing-up' the worst,
Christ became for all...'the cursed.'

While men berate Him, hurt Him, hate Him
He yet loves them, one by one:
"You'll be with me"... "I'll forgive thee,"
"Be his mother"..."be her son."

Pain unslackened, sky was blackened,
Hell was coming, very near;
Aching, breaking, God-forsaking
Jesus Christ, His Son, so dear.

Then 'twas ended, He descended,
All was mended...gone, His breath.
Love transcending, heaven blending,
Made a tunnel out of death.

Though sin's still clinging—ever stinging,
Sorrow bringing, He'll forgive.
No more "
'why'ing, fearing, crying,
Through His dying all can live.

Amazing raising, mind emblazing,
Back to life our Savior came.
Obeyed perfection, sin's correction,
RESURRECTION., Praise His name!

Just prior to the holidays, in excitingly promoting the new TV musical production of 'The Grinch Who Stole Christmas', the producer said: "We've worn out the 'Nutcracker Suite', and we've long needed a new story for Christmas, and this is it." As entertaining as these productions can be, upon hearing this, my heart achingly asked: "Whatever happened to the Original Christmas Story"? This is my response.

TRITE TIDINGS

So you're tired of that old story,
That Jesus came to save,
Was born and died for you and me,
Forever left that grave.

So it's a bore, that age old lore,
So passé, out of style:
That God's Own Mind became our kind
That He might reconcile.

This worn out Word again is heard:
Good Tidings of great joy:
"For Christ the Savior has been born,"
Messiah —God's Own Boy!

But let's update that story:
Throw in Dr. Suess's crew,
All the sugar plumb-dumb fairies,
Rabbits, elves and Santa, too.

Send in that Grinch, for it's a cinch,
When all is said and done,
He'll fill the bill; I'm sure he will,
If all you want is fun!

But, where's the Star seen from afar?
Those searching men, so wise?
Does anyone still seek Him,
Or, are most content with lies?

So this hollow way we follow
As we swallow down Vermouth,
For it seems to be so catching,
Snatching fantasy from truth.

But, I love that 'old, old story'
For ole Santa can't forgive,
Nor can Grinches, elves or fairies
Give my soul a place to live.

So don't throw out "The Baby"
With the 'watered-down-clichés'
Or let fables, tales and fantasies
Dilute your Christmas Days.

We've moved more times in our life than I'd like to admit. On one such occasion, the movers overlooked a small carrying case that I had used originally to carry my dancing shoes and exercise apparel. I had long since dispensed with the clothes, but some tap shoes and toe shoes were still there. I had added some letters from my Mother and some wartime letters from a young man, fighting in Europe, in whom I had more than a passing interest. Although I almost never went back and reread those letters, I always knew they were there. When the movers left this precious case behind, I appealed to the new home- owners, only to discover they had thrown the case and its contents into the garbage. My sense of loss amazed me.

This poem assumes that if I wanted to, I could still climb into the attic and re-experience my Mother, my career and an old flame.

It was the approach of Valentine's Day that caused me to ponder these things.

Love Letters

'Twas one of those gloomy mornings that we've all learned
to despise,
When bugles blast their reveilles, but the sun just will not rise.
So I climbed into the attic, where I store things in my mind,
And began some reminiscing, times I'm missing, left behind.

And there I see, 'midst dust debris, a treasure chest I'd hid;
I broke the lock, turned back the clock, and lifted up the lid.
This chest was filled with souvenirs from bygone years, and then
I saw these old **Love Letters** I had saved from way back when.

And with some trepidation, yet elation, I'd begun
To open up my heart and read these letters, one by one.
I'd forgotten how these words could stir my blood and
make me feel;
Because they were so personal, they had such great appeal.

The first one was from Peter, whose impulsiveness could shock.
We used to call him Reed, but he was later known as Rock.
He told me I was chosen, I was special as could be;
I'd been left a great inheritance in heaven, just for me.

The next one was from Luke, who was a doctor, I recall;
He wrote a Christmas story that was loved by one and all.
He quoted all of Jesus' Words in such Divine detail.
I felt the pounding in my heart with every pounded nail.

Then I met Paul, once known as Saul, who seemed a woman-hater;
But after I'd read all he said, I learned to love him later.
This man of steel, a former heel, could really write a letter:
"To live is Christ—to die is gain"; could this be said much better?

And then I opened one from John and must admit it's true,
This letter is my favorite, I savor it, I do.
'Twas worn out, pages torn out, 'cause I'd read it more than often.
I can't believe there's any heart this man's kind words can't soften.

Then, this one's from an older friend, Hosea was his name.
He urged me to return to God; I've never been the same.
He said each time the sun comes up, God will appear to me,
And be there, like the springtime rain, through all eternity.

Although I love these men of God who took the time to write,
I know that only Jesus gives these letters Life and Light.
So when dark looms from morning glooms,
I'll seek my treasure chest,
And read those old **Love Letters** from The One
who loves me bes**t.**

This is The Spirit of Truth that breathes new life into every hungering heart! This fact shouts "Eternal Life" to the whole world. This is the very heart of the "Good News" (Gospel). And although His death is *sufficient* to cover the sins of the whole world, it is *efficient* only to those who believe that He emptied that tomb and is alive forevermore. It's the Reason for our "Easter Excitement."

The Empty Tomb

From Mary's womb to empty tomb,
In one brief, grief-filled span,
This **Centerpiece of History**
Affected every man.

From Mary's womb to empty tomb
A painful path He trod.
In grace He grew, but no one knew
This Jesus, Jew, was God!

From Mary's womb to empty tomb
His love went "all the way".
He paid the price, while men rolled dice;
Is this still true today?

For us "to see or not to see"
He died for me is prime.
It's where "to be or not to be"
We'll spend eternal time.

From Mary's womb to empty tomb
He made our future clear:
"Because I live, you too shall live".
No greater words we'll hear.

This empty tomb dispels all gloom,
For our Dear Living Lamb
Will roll away my stone one day.
Because He is **"I Am"**

Christmas is a wonderful time of the year. And I wrote this to remind us all not to simply settle for the "temporary tinsel" of the holidays, but to celebrate the only gift that lasts all year round—the eternal presence of JESUS.

Christmas Bestivities

We all enjoy those toys and gifts,
The Christmas trees so bright.
We're fond of dear old Santa's
Bag of goodies. Such delight.

But I must ask this question
'Midst this crass commercial joy:
"Whatever did become of
Our Beloved Jewish Boy?"

I'm really all for happiness,
Love pleasure, like the rest,
But anything in place of
Always ends up second best.

That tree will drop its needles,
And its cheer will disappear.
As we pack away that "happiness"
In boxes, every year.

All that tinsel has its beauty,
But we'd better know it's brief,
'Else that failing-fast-felicity
Is apt to turn to grief.

So fill up Santa's stockings,
Feast and fill those bellies tight.
But let His love fulfill you
So your joy won't end that night.

It's when Christmas lasts forever
And our "now" becomes sublime.
It's the day when man first **Saw His Word,**
When **GOD BURST INTO TIME!**

My husband, Dr. Lane Adams, who was then pastor of a Church, was going to be preaching on "Jesus", for his Christmas message. He planned on using the song: "No Longer a Baby" to accompany his message. He wished to close with a poem, and so he asked me to write one with that subject in mind. Having the welfare of the congregation at heart—and not wishing to encourage him to preach overtime—I wrote this very short one.

(Revelation 1:4-5 "Grace and peace from Him who is, and who was, and who is to come…from Jesus Christ, who is the faithful witness, the firstborn from the dead, and the ruler of the kings of the earth").

Jesus

(No Longer a Baby)

We like to keep Him lying
In a manger or a grave,
For there His voice is silent,
No words: "obey," "behave."

Let Him grow up, this Baby,
For no one can afford
To Him just as Savior;
He must be, also, **Lord.**

This emerged from desire to put down in writing my personal gratitude to God. From a very early age on up, I had a deep need to be sure that I would live forever. I am in awe of how this has been so completely and beautifully explained to me, in His glorious Book. What a precious promise. What a "Mountain Top" message.

Isaiah 25: 6-8 "On this mountain the Lord Almighty will prepare a feast of rich food for all peoples, a banquet of aged wine—the best meats and the finest of wines. On this mountain He will destroy the shroud that enfolds all peoples, the sheet that covers all nations; He will swallow up death forever. The Sovereign Lord will wipe away the tears from all faces. He will remove the disgrace of His people from all the earth. The Lord has spoken."

CHRISTMAS FEAST

You're invited to a banquet where the Lord will be your Host.
It's an open invitation, so that no one there can boast.
You'd needn't feel you're worthy, just be searching for "The Light",
And He won't care what you wear there, just as long as it is white.

Don't bring your own-bagged-bottle, for The Lord provides the fare;
That bread and wine, His soul-food-fine, He'll serve to all who care.
Then, at this festive party, as we gather 'round "His Tree",
We'll open that great gift of joy—receive salvation, free.

For, right upon this mountain, as we wait and hold our breath,
We will get our heart's desire; He'll remove that shroud of death.
That sheet that covers nations and that veil that covers fears
Are destroyed upon this mountain, as He wipes away our tears.

Don't miss this Christmas banquet, there'll be hosts of angels there,
At this "mountain top experience" that Jesus will prepare.

Revelation 7: 13-14-17 *"...These in the white robes—who are they and where did they come from?...They have washed their robes and made them white in the blood of the Lamb...For The Lamb at the center of the throne will be their Shepherd. He will lead them to springs of living water. And God will wipe away every tear from their eyes."*

Something over three months had passed since September 11, 2001—our most recent "Day of Infamy". A pall still hung over America, and it seemed somewhat inappropriate to send greetings to celebrate Christmas. This was my effort to show the relevance of Christ and Christmas to the grief that gripped us all.

WHERE IS PEACE?

It's a difficult year to send Christmas cheer,
But what's "stable" we're able to share.
Though lives have been shattered, we've learned what has mattered.
Through rubble and trouble came "care".

Once more, in our world, many flags were unfurled,
In our fright we began to unite.
Through rage and through rancor, we looked to "Our Anchor".
And re-lit our own "Pilot Light".

We're warned that our life will continue in strife,
That this terror, no error, won't cease.
We look all around, but it just can't be found;
I'm speaking of that earthly peace.

Just where do we find what our God had in mind?
What message did Angels impart?
They were singing of peace that will ever increase
For the one who has Christ in his heart.

We're on solid ground, when **His** peace has been found,
A relationship nothing can sever.
So send Christmas cheer, anytime, any year,
He's with us both now and forever.

III.

BEHIND THE “SEENS”

My heart had broken. My soul had been seared with sadness. The fire in my life had turned to ashes. I was reaching up out of my poetic pit for some solace and hope.

FLAMENTATIONS

While gazing at my fire "embering" along its warming way,
From its flashing, flaming entrance to its exit, ashen gray,
I thought, it seems like life itself, commencing bright and gay,
Then aging gaining, draining, burning out, we pass away.

Still pondering, thoughts wandering, I faced the future, drear.
Heart sinking, I kept thinking that the end is getting near.
Then, all enthralled, I claimed, recalled God's Sweet Words:
"Have no fear. Your outward person perishes, but you will reappear."

Fear abated, hope instated, "braziered" beauty I could reap
From its flickering, heating, "hickoring", to its smoldering little heap.
Wood decreasing, "lumbering" ceasing, heavy head, I now shall creep
Toward my bed, slumbering teasing, peacefully "lay me down to sleep.

I'm finally facing a reality I should have embraced a long time ago. That is, anytime you mention God, or anything about God, you're going to inevitably end up in mystery. That's why God says in His Word: "Without faith it is impossible to please Him..." (Hebrews 11:6)

I have a mind that wants to wrap everything up with a full explanation of whatever is left dangling without an answer. When it comes down to it, you either trust God's Word and His character, or you'll go mad with the mysteries. This poem leaves a lot of things dangling, but never the necessity for faith. ("Faith is the substance of things hoped for, the evidence of things not seen." Hebrews 11:1)

I WONDER AS I WANDER

There's much about life I cannot comprehend,
Such mysteries abound from beginning to end.
I'll mention a few things—perhaps you'll agree
I find, in my mind, are the hardest to see.

The first one I hope you can help me to solve
Is "Why in the world would one want to evolve
From monkeys, which seems so demeaning and odd,
When one could choose 'made in the image of God'?"

If you can explain that, then please make this clear,
When death is the one thing we most seem to fear,
Why aren't we enthralled when we hear Our Lord say:
"Because I live, you'll live, if you'll choose MyWay?"

And then, most amazing, man's mind must embrace
That God was in Christ, when He came to our place.
So how could His Words be just 'dust on a shelf'?"
This was God reconciling the world to Himself.

This question's for Christians: I can't understand
How could we make dull all the glory God planned?
We've made "Good News" boring, His message so grim,
Or surely more people would hunger for Him.

And why would God give us His "Great Book of Facts"
Then not be aware how a man thinks or acts?
In this "game of life", He cares—He gives rules:
We play it God's way or we end up as fools.

And, how can man trust only part of God's Word?
To pick and to choose becomes quickly absurd,
For, either it's **all** true—it's ***all*** verified,
Or, none of it is—if, in part, God has lied.

But, hardest of all—I will ne'er comprehend
When thinking of Jesus, our God and our Friend,
In seeing our sinfulness, I want to know
"Just why in the world does He love us all, so?"

Romans 5:7-8
"But God demonstrates His own love for us in
this: While we were yet sinners, Christ died for us"

This was my first attempt at writing poetry. I was a new Christian and we were living in London at the time. Although I loved Jesus, I really wasn't much in touch with who I was as a person. It's one thing to know the Scriptures, but it's another thing to know yourself well enough to profitably, personally apply them. So I see this poem as a rather poignant search for "Me." (It's probably not necessary to add that I didn't write any more poetry for about another 20 years). I'm including it in the book because it makes me appreciate how faithful God has been—and still is—in leading me along The Way.

PICTURE ME

You supply the subject,
The title—call it **ME**.
My intent—to view the
Picture, theologically.

An ***image*** of the present?
Of course; but not so fast;
For much of the detail contains
A ***portrait*** of the past.

For what we are sometimes,
Or were, or might appear to be
Is captured in this ***pose***
Called "now"—***photographically***.

Do we keep **ME** right in ***focus***?
Do we have correct perspective?
Getting "both sides of the ***picture***"
Is part of my objective.

Do we see the imperfections?
Or observe less bad than good?
That our vision's very varied
Should be rightly understood.

Our parents see us young,
Although our children see us older.
So what one sees depends upon
The eyes of the beholder.

And how do others see us?
I think everybody knows.
We do not need a microscope,
Behavior really shows.

But as I look to analyze
This ***picture*** labeled **ME,**
The faces seem confused;
That's right—the faces—I see three.

The one appearing darkest, now,
Is almost hidden—"Past";
The ***proofs*** are fading quickly,
For those ***negatives*** won't last.

But, quickly then, just glance again,
You'll see another face,
"Present" is her title,
And she's so in need of grace.

Her ***visage*** changes often,
She must hover near "The Light",
Or what you see this morning
Might be different, come the night.

When drawn close to the "Spotlight"
She can really "look like sin".
Amazing, the improvement
When the "Light" shines from within.

Which brings me to my favorite face,
Photo number three:
The countenance called "future",
One that I can barely see.

It looks so very lovely,
Although the view is dim;
I like **ME** best in this one,
See how I resemble "Him".

It's the one my God has chosen,
He has picked it from all three,
Retouching it completely
That day at Calvary.

So ***focus*** on the "future",
Let's ***face*** it, it's Divine,
And we'll really "get the ***picture***"
Whether **ME** is yours or mine.

Ezekiel 36:26 "I will give you a new heart and put a new spirit in you. I will remove from you your heart of stone and give you a heart of flesh".

Luke 1:37 "For nothing is impossible with God".

YOU CAN BEGIN ANEW

The sweetest words that come from God,
Along with: "I love you",
Give a lift to the heart—a brand new start,
"You CAN begin anew."

Finding help to cope, from our God of hope
Seems too good to be true,
For, the world's lethal lore says:
"You'll be as before,
You can't shake sin's rank residue".

But, I claim it again, as I write with this pen,
Jesus' message, I need to review:
"Confess it to me, pure and clean you can be,
Try again, I love you, I do."

Watching my beautiful, talented loving mother die of Alzheimer's disease was one of the most devastating experiences of my life. Anyone who can identify with this situation will surely understand the deep heartache that is its companion. This was another past experience in my life that I tended to try and bury very deep. I finally pulled it out of its hiding place and wrote this poem. It hurt to write it and it still hurts to read it. But nothing is out of the reach of God's love. It simply pulls out of us the necessary faith to cope and trust beyond what we can understand.

I do believe this: (Job 19:25-26) "I know that my Redeemer lives and that in the end He will stand upon the earth. And after my skin has been destroyed, yet in my flesh I will see God: I myself will see Him with my own eyes—I and not another. How my heart yearns within me".

Worries and fears seem to be brought into manageable perspective in the light of this wonderful news.

CALL IT WHAT YOU WILL

I recall the day my Grandmother
Was left in Mother's keeping.
A trunk containing "all that's left"
Arrived amidst her weeping.

Her days were spent in sorrowing,
In borrowing the "past".
Her actions were confusing,
She was losing all, at last.

Ever running—even cunning,
She was simply not the same.
Always fretful, so forgetful,
Didn't even know her name.

We were shattered, all that mattered
Was reversal might take place;
No relieving, constant grieving
As we stared at "empty face".

As no other, I loved Mother,
But I watched her also fail.
I could see her, but not free her
From this coming, numbing veil.

There's no curing, so enduring
Is our temporary task.
All this "dust" can only trust
That God will give us what we ask.

Yes, I hear it, how I fear it,
I could be the next in line.
It's a testing, but I'm resting
On my loving Lord, Divine.

Call it raging, call it aging,
Call it "Alzheimer's", but still
While you're calling, call on Jesus
For it's all within His will.

I was having lunch with a friend, one day, and she began telling me about this woman who visited her often and always wore a dark cloud over her head. She lamented the fact that this "why me?-woman" did nothing but complain all the time. My friend was really being disturbed by her attitude. I happened to mention how I felt about this question: And she said: "Annette, I wish you'd write that down". So, a few years later, I did—in poetry form.

WHY ME ?

How often does God hear us whine, when things aren't fine: "Why Me?"
We cry: "Unfair! God, don't you care I'm suffering wrongfully?
You must observe I don't deserve this unjust agony;
I'm **no worse** than the average man. I must repeat: Why me?"

It's blindness to His kindness that provokes this futile plea;
This dark night sight brings on that flight to negativity.
"So let that veil be lifted, make me gifted, Lord, to see
The floodgates of your heaven that you've opened up for me."

"It's in your hands, one understands, 'to be or not to be',
And so it's just for life, itself, I thank you, gratefully.
From dust we art, in dust depart, one breath from death are we.
I'm breathing still, through your dear will and wondering: Why me?"

Just once did Jesus groan, alone and hanging on that tree,
Those haunting, wanting words: "My God, are you forsaking me?"
That wasn't fair—His dying there—so innocent was He;
That willing "mercy killing" was ordained to set us free.

How often does God hear our praise when His sweet ways we see?
In spite of us, inviting us into His family.
He's promised me a home with Him through all eternity.
No better than the average man, I must repeat: "Why me?"

Colossians 1: 15-20 **JESUS**

"He is the image of the Invisible God, the firstborn over all creation. For by Him all things were created: things in heaven and on earth, visible and invisible, whether thrones or powers or rulers or authorities; all things were created by Him and for Him. He is *before* all things. And in Him all things hold together. And He is the head of the body, the church. He is the beginning and the firstborn among the dead, so that in everything He might have the supremacy. For God was pleased to have all His fullness dwell in Him, and through Him to reconcile to Himself all things, whether things on earth or things in heaven, by making peace through His blood shed on the cross".

(Perhaps a "Praise God" would be appropriate!)

WHAT KIND OF MAN IS THIS?

As the boat becomes filled and the waters are stilled,
We are thrilled, we are chilled. Who is He?
Can just a plain man calm the waves like He can?
Please tell me, who can This One be?

I hear it's no fable, that this man is able
To heal either body or soul.
Steals years like a sleuth and renews our sweet youth,
By His Word, can make any man whole.

Now, who can give peace that is not on lend-lease,
Forgive sins and create life anew?
Perhaps, as we're told, He's some prophet of old,
Or Elijah or John—wonder who?

Does He live on this earth or is heaven His berth?
Can He really turn water to wine?
Can He hear when I pray? Is He here night and day?
Did He really say: "All power is mine?"

Who created this world, as all life was unfurled?
Was it God or His Spirit or Son?
We'd have doubt, we'd have fear, had He not come down here
To convince us that "They" are all One.

So, God, in this Form, can abate any storm
If "our boat", while afloat, goes amiss.
Yes, believe if you can, all of God's in this Man,
And you'll no longer say: "Who is This?"

(Matthew 8:27 "...What kind of man is this?
Even the winds and the waves obey Him")

One day I was reading some of the sweet Words of God: *(I John 3:1)* "How great is the love the Father has lavished on us, that we should be called children of God", or *(Matthew 23:37)* "…how often I have longed to gather you together as a hen gathers her chicks under her wings, but you were not willing," or the Scripture that triggered this particular poem, *(Jeremiah 3:19)* "…I thought you would call me 'Father' and not turn away from following me."

I was just overwhelmed with the sorrow that must fill God's heart as I contemplated all the responses to Him in our world today, which often express everything from apathy to hate. Is there anything sadder than unrequited love? I tried to enter your heart with His longings.

I THOUGHT YOU'D CALL ME FATHER

I loved you all like sons,
And wanted so for you to know;
I thought you'd call Me Father
While you lived on earth below.

I wanted you to follow Me,
To do the things I say;
I thought you'd call Me Father
And obey Me all the way.

And, oh My precious little chicks
I longed—you must have known—
To gather you beneath my wings,
Protect you as My own.

I staked out all your boundaries
To keep you from life's harms;
But you ignored My warnings,
Threw aside My Loving Arms.

I left you My inheritance,
So nothing you would lack.
Yes, ***I thought you'd call Me Father,***
But you never loved Me back.

IV.

A BIT OF WIT

At a fairly large church party, a dear friend (?) publicly presented a road map to me, with this comment: "Annette is the only person I know who can get seriously lost between the church door and the parking lot exit."

I've known the frantic fear of feeling no one will ever find me again simply because I've taken the wrong turn on a freeway. And when I exit the ladies room, in an airport, I'm almost guaranteed to turn the wrong way. Need I go on? This all finally brought me to a moment of truth—I'm "Directionally Dyslexic". (This is a term I coined to describe my wretched condition.) So I decided to deal with this dilemma by writing about it.

It is a definite handicap, but there are ways to compensate if you're creative enough—like dropping hankies along the way, spotting landmarks, or following other pretty cars—which, you've guessed, can at times go very wrong.

After sharing this poem at a party, once, I found out, to my surprise, that it's something that I seem to have in common with quite a few other people. It seems to be a deficit similar to tone deafness, and there's very little that can be done to remedy it. About the best thing I have been able to salvage, from this problem, is that I don't often get asked to drive anyone anywhere, which saves a lot of gas money. There are a few other little perks which I mention in the following lamentation.

DIRECTIONAL DYSLEXIA

I'm directionally dyslexic;
I discovered this one day.
You may follow my directions,
But just go the other way.

My poor bewildered husband
Writes directions to a spot,
But cannot understand my plight:
That backwards they work not.

Hey, I can read a road map
But I end up quite the sham,
Because I never can connect
That map to where I am.

And what's the fun in shopping
At the mall, from store to store,
If you find they are exactly where
They've always been before?

I have no trouble entering a
House by its front door;
It's leaving through their closets
That I really do abhor.

I've seen them change a street at night,
It's somehow upside-down,
And next I soon discover they've
Reversed the whole darn town.

But I feel sorry for my friends
"Wherever they do roam",
For they will never know my thrill
Of simply finding "home".

"Oh, how I've been looking forward to today; I just cannot wait to go to the dentist" is a line I'm almost positive that you'll never ever find recounted in the annals of history! So it shouldn't be hard to understand that I needed some serious outlet for the trauma I experienced, after my first adult tooth was pulled, several years ago. This poem was extracted from me shortly after recovery from that occasion.

I hope I may be forgiven for this somewhat derogatory dental diatribe which might appear to be an attack on dentists. I assure you, it is directed at the act— not the person. They must all be lovely men who simply made a miserable professional choice. What follows is my updated version of dental definitions, which, regrettably, I do not believe you will find in your basic dictionary.

DENTAL DEFINITIONS

Pulling used with Taffy makes for
Lots of fun and pleasure, but
Pulling used with ***tooth*** becomes
A day you don't quite treasure.

Drilling used with oil can be
A most rewarding venture,
While ***drilling*** put with ***tooth*** is just
The first step toward a ***denture.***

A ***hole in one*** for golfers is
A super special shot;
But a ***hole in one***, a ***mouth***, that is,
Is just an empty spot.

A ***sweet tooth*** means you love the sweets,
The cakes and candy canes.
Or your ***sweet tooth*** might just be
The only ***tooth*** that yet remains.

A ***biting mouth*** goes lashing out,
It's cutting and it irks.
Or a ***biting mouth*** could mean the one
That, gratefully, still works.

The word ***canal*** with water is
A ditch that's really grand.
Yet the word ***canal*** with ***root*** is
But your basic "last ditch stand."

A ***crown of gold*** for Christians
Is a lasting, promised truth.
But a ***crown of gold*** from dentists
Is a temporary ***tooth.***

Chewing gum in all its flavors
Is a masticating treat;
But let's hope your ***chewing gum***
Is not the means by which you eat.

A dear friend called me one day. The vibrato in her voice was a clear sign that something was very wrong. She was mortified! It seems that she had attended some women's function where someone made a remark, that triggered some past baggage she'd been toting around, and she overreacted quite vigorously! She said it was one of those reflex action moments that caused the words to simply slip out of her mouth, completely unaccompanied by any thought. She knew it would be impossible to ever go back and change it.

So, we just talked and suffered together for a while. After she hung up, I thought about her dilemma and decided to write something that might rub a little balm on her open emotional sore. It's surely a situation that, unfortunately, we can **all** identify with; and a little humor can sometimes go a long way towards lightening the load.

A SLIP OF THE LIP

A "slip of the lip"—what a hazardous trip!
How we fret, we regret what we've said.
Those words are imbedded and cannot be shredded,
We sometimes could wish we were dead.

We simply don't think, then, as quick as a wink,
We might bark a remark, without plan;
No way to save face and no way to erase
All those words that will then "hit the fan".

We've all known that drain from a deep "faux pas" pain,
(That's assumin' we're human, in race).
For our own "tongues of fire" will all soon require
His mind-bending, kind-mending grace.

His Word even shows He'll make peace with our foes,
'Can defeat or delete any blips.
And everyone knows, He could end all our woes
If He simply would zip up our lips.

(Psalm 141: "Set a guard over my mouth, O Lord;
keep watch over the door of my lips).

Someone has stated: "Whoever made up that term for older people—"The Golden Years"— must have been colorblind. Although that line has some merit and could be construed as a "laugh or cry" situation, I chose to have some fun with it. Enjoy—through your tears.

THOSE MOLDIN', GOLDEN YEARS

When did that "bright and shiny" face
Take on a greasy look?
It seems to happen overnight,
Our youth has been forsook.

When did our hair first start to roam,
Completely lose its place?
It peaks out, sneaks out ears and nose,
'Seems out to conquer face.

When does our epidermis thin
And just give-in to stress?
Forget the clothes, when ironing,
It's skin we need to press.

Is "pucker up and kiss me"
Now a needless proposition,
'Cause our lips are now positioned
In that permanent condition?

'Can't even trust our words, for
Meanings change with passing time:
What now they're calling "age spots"
Were "cute freckles" in our prime.

When did a simple errand
To a room that's very near,
Become a task that makes us ask:
"Let's see, why am I here?"

And when did they start asking
Stupid questions at the store,
Like: "Want your senior discount?
May I help you out the door?"

Does "Come to bed and sleep with me",
That captivating tease,
Now often mean just one more night
Of catching up on "ZZZZZ"s?

When did our flesh all splay, betray,
And make us feel bereft,
'Cause muscles strong, we had so long
Have now just up and left?

When "blush on" comes from "brush on",
Not because of what was said,
Just color our face grateful,
Though we're pale, we're not yet dead.

When did small things start hiding,
Make themselves so hard to find,
Like our glasses, keys and wallets?
Next, I'm sure I'll lose my mind.

Well, one thing is a positive,
So something's going right.
No need to buy eye shadow,
It appears with morning light.

"Old age is not for sissies"
Is a line one often hears,
But, trade it"? Hey, we made it
To these "moldin', golden years.

We hadn't owned a dog since our daughter was married over thirty years ago. But now that we weren't traveling much anymore, we were giving it some thought. We would vacillate between "Oh, it would be such fun" to "Ugh, do we really want to get ourselves involved in all that responsibility and expense again?"

It was while we were in that "California state of mind" that we went to visit our daughter, in Maryland. She encouraged us to look around, which we did. Our "dog shopping" was less than successful when, as a last straw, we stopped at a Pet Store in a Mall. Well, there, peeking out at us from behind those cruel wired-in walls was the cutest little bundle of white "cotton candy" on four legs I'd ever seen. Two coal black eyes and a black nose was all that made him look real. (We've had people say to us: "He looks like a toy"). I melted on the spot. It happened to be April 1st, and I was certainly making a fool of myself. Good sense and wisdom didn't even enter into the picture from then on.

We had to leave him there for a few days while he got all his shots. (Of course we visited him every day). When we finally left for the airport with him to return home to California, we were quite the sight—puppy dog, carrying case, dog house, toys, food, instructions—the works. Of course we had to buy him a plane ticket, and then they unfairly forced him to stay under the seat. He was so good all the way home that nobody even knew we had a dog with us.

In trying to decide what to name him, while eating in a restaurant, our waitress happened to mention that she had a huge Rottweiler named Muldoon. My husband said: "That's it". So we have a little 15 pound Bichon Frise named Muldoon, whom we really adore. I wanted him to have a place in my book as well as in my heart.

"BONE"A FIDE(O) BEAUTY

"The Mighty Muldoon" touched our lives none too soon,
We sought him and bought him, one day.
This "handful of fuzz" made us love him becuz
He chose us—demanded to stay!

He's a Bichon Frise—as his papers display,
One of Royalty's most precious things.
All his wishes unhampered, he scampered, was pampered,
And carried on pillows by Kings.

He's a white ball of fluff, like a soft furry muff,
And his hair he will ne'er ever shed.
But you're right in assuming his high cost of grooming,
It's his monthly upkeep we dread.

His hair is demanding—requiring a "standing"
On each month—a shampoo and cut.
We might have been smart, if we'd known from the start
And chosen a bald-headed mutt.

He dribbles a ball like those athletes so tall,
He taunts as he flaunts his great moves.
"When all's said and done", that boy's made for fun,
And each day his playing improves.

And talk about rest—our Muldoon's at his best,
To disturb him one couldn't be ruder,
But a sound at the door, and he's up fighting for:
His homeland—"repel the intruder"!

He loves to hear singing, all music starts bringing
That tale-wagging-happy-faced-smile.
His mother was "Dancy", his father was "Rowdy",
His heritage gives him his style.

I was simply appalled by this story, recalled:
A puppy—one so small in size,
His proud owner said: "He is just out of bed;
He had implants put into both eyes."

My judgment, so clear, moved into high gear,
"That's going too far," I decried.
"In my day we bred them, we loved them and fed them,
But when they got sick they just died."

Then, 'Doon got injections for bad ear infections,
My own words, I ate—I had sinned.
When we got our bill, though our heart's just stood still,
My righteous stand "went with the wind".

A dumb bell he ain't, and although he's no Saint
His training caused no strain or fuss.
But then came a switch, that cute "son of a bitch"—
Muldoon—ended up training ***us***!

Our son-in-law, T.M. Moore, is a poet in the most classic sense of the word. In one year, he had poems published in thirteen different publications. For years he has urged me to branch out beyond the ballad form I am addicted to, but all to no avail. His poem to me, THE BALLAD TAMER, in the Foreword of this book, is his kind surrender to my permanent love of the ballad. This poem was written while I was still trying to convince him that I would ever be a balladeer.

THE METER MAID

Just between Big T. and little ol' me,
I simply can't hack that (per)verse they call free.
So, back in my driver's seat, causing despair
Is that sweet, banal, ballad beat sitting right there.

Now T.'s pen doth march to correct cadence time,
Delighting, while writing his content in rhyme.
He will change, rearrange, make his message complete,
Walking into our hearts on (big) poetic feet.

Well, a ballad is valid, I guess one can say,
(In defending my ending up writing this way),
A Shakespeare, it's quite clear, I won't become soon,
But I love 'making time' with that old ballad tune.

I've tried to improve, but these old 'feet' won't move,
Gone amuck, I seem stuck in that grandmother groove.
For what does "iambic", pen pal of "pentameter",
Mean to this meter maid, renegade amateur?

My husband and I had decided to give our son-in-law four new tires for his birthday gift. (He travels so much he was practically riding on rims). So I wrote this little ditty to accompany the gift. It's a "pun"ny poem.

WRITTEN WITH *RIM* AND REASON

We hear you soon plan to re***tire,***
Your ***odometer*** shows your old age.
You sure ***auto*** know, a ***car*** will not go
If you ***rubber*** wrong, now, at this stage.

We ***flat*** out won't ***skid*** you one bit,
Our goal is to ***spare*** you some care.
If we can but help you ***tread*** water,
And aid in a little ***repair***.

Our aim is to ***jack*** up your burdens,
Inflate, elevate how you feel.
Just ***align-ment*** and sent most sincerely,
To ***drive*** home—we love our "Big ***Wheel***

Written after having been treated to the most marvelous medley of songs a bird-lover would ever want to hear.

A *TRILL*-OGY

I have season tickets
To a "concert on the green".
I've the best seat in the house,
It's called a window box with screen.

The house lights now are dimming
As the curtains pull apart.
They're tuning up their instruments,
The show's about to start.

I hear tweeting, warbling, chirping,
It's a bird-fest, you have guessed,
All the trilling is so thrilling,
It's surround-sound at its best.

I looked for all those singers
But while searching got a blow:
It's a shocking word, but a mockingbird
Puts on this one-man-show.

He can imitate, he can titillate,
All these antics he enjoys.
I can hear him say, at the end of day:
"OK, let's take five, boys"!

Now when I hear this chorus
Singing for us—though absurd,
Although I speak in jest,
He could be best of "all the bird".

V.

ETERNAL EXPECTATIONS

Surely His goodness and mercy *have* followed me all the days of my life. The very first time I saw the mountains of California I was thrilled beyond measure. But, as usual, we soon had to move elsewhere. It seemed almost impossible to me that we could ever return to California again; but, of course I learned once more that "Nothing is impossible with God"(Matthew 20:26), for here I am. And I'm still filled with wonder each day to find myself here.

We now live on top of a mountain and have a glassed in area on the view side of our house. Each morning as I awaken, my eyes are fairly assaulted with the wonders of His creation…a 180 degree view of mountain ranges almost to Mexico. Besides human residents there are also many precious animal and bird families who have homes on and about this real estate.

Upon beholding these magnificent marvels of creation, Scripture cannot help but invade one's thoughts: "The earth is the Lord's and the fullness thereof…the world, and they that dwell therein" (Psalm 24:1). Each day I appreciate anew His love that brought me out here.

This poem was such fun for me to write.

MORNING GLORY

I awoke again this morning
To view mountains wrapped in foam,
To see scruffy little cactus plants
That badly need a comb.

The desert dew is busy
Basting grass and trees anew;
I drink deeply of this beauty
As I drink my coffee brew.

The humming birds are droning—
Honing in on every bloom
As they tread the air and sip the fare
In God's great dining room.

The ground around starts moving
As the animals draw near.
They preen and glean, that sweet routine
Which says: "I'm glad I'm here."

I glimpse a baby rabbit
Sporting new translucent ears,
As he nibbles very neatly,
Then discreetly disappears.

The desert drunk, Road Runner,
Is, as always, "in his cup."
He'll never know which way to go
Or know which way is up.

The coyote night time prowler,
If still hungry, then stalks by.
His days are grim, survival slim;
We stole his land, that's why.

What's this? They quickly dart and
All depart, remain so still;
"The reason" then comes swooping down,
The hawk is on the kill.

And then I spot a sparrow,
Color drab, no claim to fame.
But when he falls, we know God calls
That feathered friend by name.

But the beauties of creation, seen
With all God's love adorning,
Just won't compare to what waits there
When I awake, one morning.

I'm sure that like all of you, Scriptures that have meant one thing to me all my life, will suddenly leap out and give me an additional insight that never occurred to me before.

Can being "locked out" ever bring a good feeling?

LOCKED OUT

We've been ***locked out*** of houses,
But that's nothing new.
We've been ***locked out*** of cars
With the keys in full view.

We know what it's like
To be ***locked out*** of choice,
Where politics reign and
We're left with no voice.

We know what it's like
Being 'out of the loop',
Locked out, kept from feeling
A part of the group.

Being ***locked*** from a door
We've agreed, we appall;
When the door's to a heart
It's the worst thing of all.

Then one day we start
Being ***locked out*** by age,
Our senses start fading,
We're on the last page.

But, this time we're happy,
If we've understood.
This time we're blessed
Being ***locked out*** <u>for good.</u>

For Christ reassures us
With Words we know well:
"I, alone, hold the keys that
Lock <u>you</u> *out* of hell."

Revelation 1: 17-18
"Fear not: I am the first and the last. I am He that liveth and was dead, and behold I am alive forevermore. And I hold the keys to hell and death".

It's so easy to get hung up in rituals and rules and miss the sweet simplicity of why God made us human beings the way He did. As one contemplates the word "love" we have to know it's a unique word. With enough power you can make other people do a lot of things. You can make them obey you; you can force them to repeat words of respect, like "sir" or ma'am"; you can make them behave certain ways through fear. But the one thing you cannot force them to do is *love* you.

If God had wanted to, He could have made us all loving Him—like robots. But have you noticed He never forces Himself on any of us? He elected to give us free choice to reject or receive Him, so that when He hears the words "I love you", He would know that came of our own volition.

Doesn't Hosea 6:3 and 6 (Living Bible Version) just tear at your heart: "Oh, that we might know the Lord! Let us press on to know Him, and He will respond to us as surely as the coming of dawn or the rain of early spring…I don't want your sacrifices—I want your love; I don't want your offerings—I want you to know me."

He is so easy to love!

REMEMBER ME

I don't recall Him saying:
"Build huge structures all can see,
Or erect imposing monuments
So you'll remember Me".

"Those superficial statues
Bring a stench I want to flee;
Just read my Word & keep it,
Then I'll know that you love Me".

"I hate your empty rituals;
It's mercy I would see.
When you do it unto others,
Child, you do it unto Me".

I do recall Him saying,
Just before He went above,
"Eat this bread, my body broken,
It's a token of my love.

And also sup this cup,
It represents blood shed for thee.
It's no great task; but this I ask:
With love, remember Me."

We've all experienced "heartburn" from eating rich food, but how often have we known "heartburn" from eating Soul food— the Words of Jesus?

The Word says in Luke 24:32 "…"Did not our heart burn within us, while He talked with us by the way, and while He opened to us the Scriptures?

Matthew 26:39 "…And He went a little farther, and fell on His face, and prayed, saying, O my Father, if it be possible, let this cup pass from me: nevertheless not as I will but as thou wilt." What loving obedience!

Who can come anywhere close to feeding on these words of Scripture and not get "heart-burn"?

THE FULL CUP

His cup was full of suffering.
Of buffering the world.
He was smitten, as was written,
Curses shouted, hatred hurled.

He prayed His cup be taken,
He was shaken, faced the end;
This cup was filled with fury,
Just a jury, not a friend.

His flesh did wilt beneath our guilt,
He sank, He drank the cup.
His blood was spilled, just as God willed,
His own life He gave up.

He now "prepares a table",
Sets our blessed breakfast tray
With a FULL CUP running over,
For He emptied His that day

This is a conversation with God. I included many questions I once had myself, and some I've heard others ask.

All my life I'd been seeking for assurance of heaven, wondering why it escaped me. My eager inquiries always centered on other people. I somehow expected them to say a magic word that would turn on my light. It was not until I realized that no other human being could give me that confidence that I finally turned to the appropriate source. It was when I read Jeremiah 29:13-14a that I began searching in the right place. It says, there: "And you shall seek Me, and find Me, when you shall search for Me with all your heart. And I will be found of you, saith the Lord..."

The last part of my poem evidences that God keeps His promises. It is never the word of men that can bring assurance to the heart, it is always the Word of God.

FOREVER ME

Dear God:

Confused and empty, I cry out,
But what shall my voice cry?
There's so much I don't understand;
Why life, when we but die?

I know I am as grass, alas,
A flower soon to fall.
Like lawn, I'm gone; I'll wither;
Is there any point at all?

Who comprehends your mind, Oh, God?
Our end seems so obscure.
I'm in ebb-tide years, on a sea of fears;
Is anything for sure?

My question, God, if it's allowed
(There's no way I can fake it)
Is heaven real? That's my appeal;
And will I ever make it?

Why can't I know where I will go?
I want, I wish, I grope so.
To find my space, my resting place,
It's not enough to hope so.

I've heard You are forever, God.
But what is that to me?
It's I, myself, who wants to last,
To live eternally.

Dear Annette:

Be silent, I will answer thee,
My Word is where you'll find
The answer to your crying heart,
Both yours and all mankind.

It's all arranged, I've never changed,
"I AM", I speak what's true.
And because I live outside of time
It means that so can you.

I entered earth, in Jesus' birth,
I only stayed awhile.
I underwent your punishment
So we could reconcile.

I lived for you, I died for you,
Then I regained My breath.
I showed you how to come to me
So you could conquer death.

Dear God:

You don't deceive, I do believe
That what you say is true.
I'm glad I wasn't put on earth
Without a Word from You.

Expendable or "end"able,
Praise God, I'll never be.
My body must return to dust,
But, I'm **Forever Me**.

Imagine moving into the area of Knoxville, Tennessee and experiencing the worst winter that most people could ever remember. And this, after having lived ten years in the warm, sunny, North County of San Diego, California. I had begun to feel like winter would never end as I stared at leafless, lifeless trees with the only encouragement being a handful of evergreens. By faith alone could I believe that spring would ever come.

BOUGH IN WORSHIP

Some barren branches spoke to me
As I looked out today.
A wearied winter plodded on
Through snow, through rain, through gray.

A chilling breeze attacked the trees,
Which seemed to me so rude.
They shivered and they quivered,
For their limbs were all stripped nude.

They said to me: "We may look dead,
Or brittle, stiff and dry,
But we do learn as seasons turn
Our roots don't ever die.

Just staring at our bleak, black bough
No man could ever guess
This outfit isn't permanent,
We'll soon be in full dress."

We humans, too, know dormant days,
Discouragement, despair,
When all we see is sin's debris
Abounding everywhere.

But we can be just like that tree
And stand in time of strife,
When our roots, too, are planted in
God's weathered Words of Life.

The "outward man doth perish"
As the seasons come and go,
Yet the inner man, well grounded,
Does still grow. How good to know.

Those barren branches spoke to me
As I looked out today:
"He will revive, keep me alive"
For spring is on its way.

John 11:25-26 "Jesus said unto her, I Am the resurrection and the life: he that believeth in me though he were dead, yet shall he live; and whosever liveth and believeth in me shall never die..."

VI.

WHEN FRIENDS COME TO MIND

I have a dear friend, Dr. Doris Morgan, whose father, Reverend Vernon Byron, a minister, had one of the saddest childhoods that one could possibly imagine. Although he had a home, and his mother allowed him to stay there, she never acknowledged him as her son. No one ever understood why. So all his life he ached to be loved and longed to know that he belonged to a family. I, personally, only spent one evening with him, but I can honestly say that he was one of the meekest, kindest, most tenderly humble men I have ever known.

He was also a very talented wood carver, so before he died he spent a long time carving large, beautiful Grandfather clocks for each one of his children. He wanted to leave something of himself behind to be present…standing in the midst of them…so they would never forget that he was a part of them.

When he died I wrote this poem for my friend, Doris, in honor of her dear, loving father.

THE GRANDFATHER CLOCK

I'll never again see a Grandfather Clock
And behold it as I did before:
Just ticking off time, or ringing a chime,
One bought from a furniture store.

For I've seen a clock that was made by hand
With a love that is hard to find,
By a teacher, a preacher, a father, a friend,
A carpenter humble and kind.

Here was a man, so sad as a lad,
'Spent haunting, love-wanting days,
'Had a roof overhead, but none ever said:
"I'll love you, my son, always."

So he did all he could, as he fashioned from wood
The clocks that just might right the wrong.
And he gave them away to his family to say:
"Please know I so need to belong".

No, I'll never again see a Grandfather Clock
As just standing in space on a floor.
It stands for this loving man's living—his giving,
It stands for what God has in store:

For now he no longer is "carving out time",
He is in his **grand** ***Father's*** embrace,
And he finally knows what it's like to belong
In God's perfect and permanent place.

Alice McIntire was a wealthy lady who lived in Rancho Santa Fe, California. She had opened her lovely home to teach a Bible class for women in her area for over fifty years. Her ministry opened the door for many of them to come to love the Lord.

She also had many elaborate parties and Teas, which always had the purpose of bringing glory to God. She was a very unique and fascinating lady with a marvelous sense of humor. She had an array of wigs and hats you wouldn't believe, and was always dressed to the hilt. Her home was decorated with angels everywhere, and she had a beautiful collection of teacups from all over the world. She was truly "the hostess with with the mostest". Everyone loved her.

During the last few years of her life she was almost completely blind (from a disease known as Macula Degeneration). This never caused her to miss one step in her life goal—which was to turn people's hearts to Christ. She continued teaching her Bible class—with the help of a good friend and Bible teacher, Betty Taflinger—until she died at age 92, in 1997. I still cannot drive past her street without feeling an ache of emptiness in my heart. I really miss her.

I was asked to conduct her Memorial Service, which more than one hundred people attended, coming from all over the United States. I closed the service with the reading of this poem, which I'd written in her honor. She was unforgettable!

WHEN ALICE COMES TO MIND

When Alice comes to mind
I think of every pretty thing:
Of roses, and of tea cups,
And of angels on the wing.

She'd seldom let you see her
Without that wondrous blend
Of dress and hair and makeup,
A woman to the end.

She modeled all those pretty clothes
And loved them, we'll admit;
But what she modeled best for us
Is that she never quit.

The fact that she was feisty
Is much more than just a rumor,
'Twas the heart of, a great part of
Her delightful sense of humor.

She filled her home with treasures,
But they never could compare
To the treasure without measure,
Stored in heaven, waiting there.

We've seen the end of parties,
Bible classes, and her "Teas",
But we'll never see the end of what
God wrought through all of these.

She was mediator, teacher,
She would pray and help you mend.
She was counselor or critic.
She was Alice. She was friend.

Though her eyes had lost their vision,
They had never lost His Light.
And now she sees Him face to face
With faultless, perfect sight.

We all knew how she longed, O Lord,
To "meet you in the air".
But you, instead, came to her bed;
How sweet, You met her there.

Right up until the very end,
Her heart was still on fire
For Jesus, whom she loved so much,
Our Alice McIntire.

Who would dare to call a renowned missionary nurse "The Desert Rat"? But I entitled my biography of Aileen Coleman that way because that's what she insists on calling herself. This poem was written to explain the name and her mission.

She simply would not tolerate the title "Angel of the Desert," which had been given her in a highly complimentary *Qantas In Flight Magazine* article. Nor would she allow anyone to refer to her as Dame Aileen Coleman, after Queen Elizabeth of England conferred that title on her with the Order of Australia. This honor was bestowed on her because of her forty years of service to tubercular Bedouin in the Middle East. My book, *The Desert Rat* is all about her remarkable life. I began and ended the book with this poem.

THE DESERT RAT

(Aileen Coleman)

At the opening of her Biography:

An "Angel of the Desert",
Her admirers named her that.
But ask her what she calls herself,
You'll hear: "The Desert Rat".

She seems much like the rest of us,
Her needs, her loves, her heart;
Yet, observing her in action
Truly sets her far apart.

Success to her's not numbers,
Big crowds of humankind.
It's healing, loving Bedouins,
That "one lost sheep" she'll find.

I long to tell her story.
I'm about to "tip my hat"
To this "Angel of the Desert"
That she calls "The Desert Rat".

At the closing of her Biography:

Abraham's tent she longs to fill,
Will ne'er be satisfied
Till each lost sheep—till every child
Of Ishmael is inside.

An "Angel of the Desert",
We can all agree on that.
But, ask her what she calls herself,
It's still "The Desert Rat".

From the very first moment I met Zorica (Dawn Joy), I felt an almost unreal love well up in my heart. I met her around 1985, and then we left California within that year. Even though I'd moved away, our friendship continued until we returned to California, to retire, in 1992. It has been a special relationship through the years, in which we have shared many joys and sorrows.

The Lord Jesus walked into her life, in the late 80's, and changed her more quickly and completely than any other person I'd ever known. It was a "Joy" to behold. She hungered for and fed on His Word, daily. Everything else took a back seat, for over two years, everything except serving God.

Then God put Duff in her life and they were married in 1995. What a "match made in heaven" that has been.

A most amazing thing occurred in September of 1998. Inspired by her artist mother-in-law, she picked up a brush and tried her hand at painting, which she'd never done before in her life. She was given an almost instant amazing talent, which has brought her many awards and many first prize ribbons, in the Escondido Art Association. She has now reached the level of Masters. And she has been accepted into the exclusive La Jolla, CA Art Association. She has completed over 200 paintings since September of '98. All of this and she's been painting barely four years. It truly is a miracle. She especially loves to paint roses—the subject of most of her award-winning works of art.

As a gift, I framed a newspaper picture of her holding her first place "Rose" painting, and added this poem, in the frame, underneath her photo.

A ROSE

Our God's great creation fills all with elation,
What beauty our Lord did compose,
And what's more serene than the peace that is seen
In the grace of – the face of – ***a rose.***

The petals, demure, with their curving allure
All whisper: "Please look but don't feel,
For my thorns stand guard, as I bask in the yard,
Protecting my fragile appeal."

A rose, when it goes, leaves a stench in the nose,
An aroma of life that has perished,
But Dawn sees her duty to keep all this beauty
That all of our eyes have so cherished.

Thus she will conserve, she will paint, will preserve
On canvas—the life of **a rose.**
Her paint brush will render, retain all the splendor
Forever, in one "still life" pose.

God's great masterpiece (and His work will not cease)
Is Zorica—His fine work of art.
We've all seen her "flower", from the very first hour
That Jesus **arose** in her heart.

Duff Joy is one of our very best friends. While we were still in California, he lived only four houses away from us. (He happens to be married to my dearest friend, Dawn). He is the kind of man you read about in fairy tales, but seldom meet in real life. HE CAN FIX EVERY-THING! Not only is he *able* to fix it—he *does* fix it. He's always only a phone call away. (We're beginning to reach for the phone when we can't get the top off a jar). He manages to do this even though his business schedule always involves long working hours each day.

But what is even more important is that he's a great man of God. He is there for you in any kind of trouble—ready to pray and help.

I wrote this poem for him and gave it to him for Christmas, one year. I put in it a frame that was decorated with every imaginable kind of tool. Although it was kind of cute, putting it in a big heart frame might have been even more appropriate.

DUFF

He's a worker for God
Who has honed all His **tools,**
In his labors of love
He has followed God's **rules.**

He **lifts** heavy burdens,
Repairing the soul,
As he "**hammers** home" truth
That can make a man whole.

He **paints** a clear picture,
He **measures** God's Word,
He **drills** home the message—
The Best ever heard.

This man's not for hire,
No one could afford
To pay for his service;
He works for his Lord.

(Ephesians 2:10)

The loveliest couple used to live next door to us, Ed and Kathy Lanzara. (They have since moved away). They were expecting their first child.

I have never seen anyone prepare their home or their hearts like this couple. I think Ed planted a new variety of flowers on their patio about every other day. And if even a stray leaf happened to appear anywhere, it was immediately swept away. "Mr. Clean" could have moved right in and felt at home.

They were constantly painting inside and out; you could see baby furniture arriving on the scene; and the anticipation on their faces burst forth in the happiest of smiles, continually. So I wrote this little poem by way of rejoicing with them over the coming blessed event.

MATTHEW

A miracle is taking place,
It's one we can't ignore.
A great event, this child, God-sent,
Is coming right next door.

This boy that they're expecting
Is affecting all they do;
The changes they are making, undertaking,
All are new.

The patio's antiseptic,
So 'well keptic'—squeaky clean,
A brick floor's newly laid, for which they paid
A lot of 'green'.

Such beauty rims the edges,
Flowered hedges catch the eye.
They bask there, primed, it's all been timed
To welcome this young guy.

Their rooms they're renovating
As they're waiting for this joy;
Preparing both their home and hearts
To nurture this dear boy.

And God will say: "Dear Matthew,
On this path you daily take,
If this by-way will be MY-way
No better choice you'll make."

"I've picked two precious parents
Who will love you from your birth.
But my love lasts forever,
Goes beyond your time on earth".

When Ed and Cathy see your face
Their hearts will tell them, then:
God's made no other just like you,
And never will again.

This poem is practically self-explanatory. I wrote it right after having received a thoughtful, timely, and encouraging letter from a good friend.

LONG DISTANCE LOVE

Have you ever received a kiss and a hug,
A pick-me-up, a warm heart tug?
A listening ear, a face-to-face,
Compassion galore, responding grace?

Is there anything much better?

Only when affectionate love,
As mentioned in the lines above
Is hindered not by miles between,
Lets time, lets nothing intervene

And comes by phone or letter.

VII.

ALL IN THE FAMILY

I wrote this to our daughter, Susie, inviting her to take a very short journey through her years spent at home. It is hard to believe that those days are over. But it is such nice nostalgia—such joy and sweet sorrow. How grateful I am to have had the privilege of raising her and now seeing her move on into her own world. She is such a wonderful woman of God and such a super mother and grandmother.

How quickly the years do vanish. (I think I've heard that somewhere before...). The song, from "Fiddler On The Roof", really says it all: "Sunrise, sunset, sunrise, sunset, swiftly flow the years...one season following another, mingled with happiness and tears..."

A MOTHER'S MEMORIES

I once had a baby, most surely, not maybe,
I'd never done this thing before.
I carried, she tarried, I finally ferried
This cute, crying cargo ashore.

While I was still woozie, I named this girl Susie,
This bundle of blue-eyed delight.
I fed her, I led her and, often, I read her
A story or two every night.

I trained her, restrained her, and often disdained her
Desire to acquire her own way.
'Twas all part of growing, of knowing and showing,
That "I-am-me" daily display.

Her concept of money was, first, very funny:
Allowances frittered away.
I'd question her thinking, and then, without blinking,
"Use it, 'fore ya lose it", she'd say.

She soon didn't spend it and learned she could lend it,
The tables were turned, we got burned.
When needing to borrow, we found, to our sorrow
We'd pay back, plus interest she'd earned.

Her first sight of city, New York, what a pity,
At five she was "hushed, crushed and bossed."
She said: "It's a fact, that these people all act
Like they've just played a game and they've lost."

She saw this stray, Buddy, all beat up and bloody,
She fed him, so he hung around.
He gave her affection and loving protection,
The best dog that she ever found.

Though cute as could be he had no pedigree,
Yet she preened him for dog-show-display.
To our great surprise, Buddy got 2nd Prize,
He'd won for "Good Manners", that day.

Her parakeet pet was as smart as they get,
"Pal" could mimic each word that he heard.
But I must admit, when he flew his last "flit",
Not a tear did appear for that bird.

Her memory's fine, almost elephantine;
She will never forget this "bad news":
I set out to miss her, but hit her sweet "kisser";
Her crying brought "buying of shoes."

Her Dad was a teacher, a traveling preacher,
Was well-known as our-long-gone-Lane.
So, we were together through all kinds of weather,
Through illness, strong-willness and rain.

But there were those bright rays, those talk-through-the-night-days,
The times when the bonding was done.
We did lots of shopping, and lopping, corn-popping;
I still often miss all that fun.

Soon <u>our</u> days were numbered, she was so encumbered
With college and knowledge and men.
But God then went deeper; I knew He would keep her,
'Twas simply a matter of "when."

She changed her direction and knew some rejection,
But, faithfully, emptied her hand.
God began to replace in that vacuous space
That full life He'd long ago planned.

And, next we will find her, ("he wined and he dined her")
At that Christian Campus out West,
This "he" is "Big T", he was obviously
"Teeing-off" on his quest for "the Best."

I did fail to mention, ('twas not my intention)
How she paid her way – what a "bummer."
During days she was seen cleaning up each latrine,
In that "purge-the-pot-Camelot-summer."

This led to that whirl, wedding plans for my girl;
Needed grace, just to face this new life.
"What had happened to years?" I did question through tears,
As <u>one</u> faintly, hears: "...man and wife."

I smiled, I did act, that veneer never cracked
While I hosted, then toasted the bride.
When I saw her leave, then I started to grieve;
I could no longer keep it inside.

Her marriage did bloom, with the fruit of her womb,
I thought I had taught her "the score".
She forgot all my words 'bout "the bees and the birds"
And ended up having four "Moore."

Then, life did unsettle, God tested her mettle,
And she has come through, solid gold.
Like a strong olive tree, though it's small, you can see
Through the gales, it prevails, as foretold.

Her children have grown, begun lives of their own,
And as God moves the hands on His clock;
I'm filled with elation, that each generation
Is grounded, still founded on "ROCK."

Though time passes fast, it's the memories that last,
And this one will brighten my night:
Yes, I had a baby, most surely, not maybe,
My Susie, my blue-eyed delight.

Quite a few years prior to my writing this, I happened to say to my son-in-law, T.M. Moore, that I'd had two lines going through my head for the longest time. I simply could not find the format in which to use them. T. M. commented that he liked them very much.

So, about five years later, I decided to use them and frame them in a poem dedicated to him. It was an effort to give him an insight into the person that helped to form the girl he chose to marry.

"IT ISN"T THAT YOU DO NOT CARE; IT'S SIMPLY THAT YOU WERE NOT THERE"

I've turned a page and reached that stage,
The one that follows "middle age":
When we begin to scrutinize
Those years that pass before our eyes.

So *lend* your ear, with *interest* hear
A brief review of yesteryear.
Though other lives will quite outshine,
I like this life because it's mine.

And, no offence, in any sense,
If I should lose my audience.
I'll know it's not that you don't care;
It's simply that you were not there.

First years are blurred, not much occurred;
'Twas mainly fear I overheard:
Depression words, like "crash, "despair",
I'm grateful, glad you were not there.

No Welfare State to compensate;
Friends took us in and filled our plate.
I know 'twas kind of them to share,
But I felt shame; life seemed unfair.

Next came the drive—achieve, survive;
My dancing helped me stay alive.
I entertained; I taught in schools;
I reached my goals; I kept the rules.

Then dark clouds grew, came World War II.
Men-gone-so-long was all we knew.
Our world today seems unaware
Of freedom's price, paid "Over There."

Next, lots of fun, an honor won:
My senior year had just begun.
I went to "one large school", I'm told,
Four thousand students were enrolled.

Won't minimize my great surprise
When I was picked by all those guys
To be their sponsor—march and stand
Beside that National Champion Band.

The war, unrest, our trip out West
Was cancelled at the school's behest.
Instead, the band took trips each day
To play as soldiers marched away.

They left by train—not aeroplane,
Just one big station, filled with pain.
I'll not forget those crowds, those cries;
"The Band Played On" through sad "good-byes".

My dance career then 'got in gear',
Success, no less, seemed crystal clear.
I had a certain savoir-"flaire";
I kinda wish that you'd been there.

Too soon my life just fell apart—
A "wounded knee", a broken heart.
Would all I'd get from work and sweat
Be damaged dreams and great regret?

A time to live—a time to die.
A time to dance—a time to cry.
(I'll later learn: with death there'll be
New body parts—with warranty).

Then enter Lane, my singing swain,
Who led me into new terrain.
'Bout this affair your bound to care:
You'll "loot the fruit" from this ripe pair.

"New life" was sent—that great event,
Came Susie—no equivalent.
How swift, the years spent with our girl,
God's precious gift, that priceless pearl.

Then enter God, who made me whole:
He just exploded in my soul.
And this "New Life" is something rare;
My search for heaven ended there.

With "Susie's Choice" I had no voice,
But you must know how I rejoice.
And through the years I've shown I care
By simply, seldom being there!

You must detect how I respect
Your discipline and intellect.
You're talented, but most of all
In "faithfulness" you *stand so tall.*

Then, marriage strains, those dreaded drains,
Those after-birth-post-*pardon*-pains,
Could I repeat, I'd change—delete
Those "years I let the locusts eat."

But, here's the rest, how I've been blest;
These "golden years" are just the best.
We're "on the brink", there's more to get;
Just think, "We ain't seen nothin' yet."

I've skimmed through years and trimmed the tears,
But add this to your patient ears:
It's never that **HE** does not care;
Our great **"I AM"** was always there!

I wrote this to our daughter, Susie, on Mother's Day—1994. She had been made to feel less than "successful" because she'd opted to be a stay at home mother to raise their four children. (These were the days when a lot of women would say: "What do you do all day?" if you didn't work out of the house in a paying job). Try raising four children and you'll learn the real definition of work. Since then, I do believe that people are beginning to see some of the sad results in the "latch key" generation.

But I wrote this poem to encourage her in the fact that she had made the right decision where God was concerned.

MOTHER TO MOTHER

No usable credentials
Of monetary worth,
A dossier that empty
Twenty years from baby's birth.

We hear: "No higher calling…",
Those pulpit pearls of praise,
But others say: "What **do** you do?
How do you spend your days?"

It's when we look to God, Who
"Wrote the Book" on what's worthwhile,
We strive to be the Mother
Who will make "Our Father" smile.

And, opening up that "final file",
Our "dossier Divine",
He'll say: "You've got credentials,
All essentials—you are Mine."

This was written right after my daughter, Susie, returned home, following an all-too-short visit.

I'm sure there's not a mother anywhere in the world who has never experienced the deafening silence, that almost suffocates, in this aftermath. The empty-house-heaviness that pervades heart and home is really indescribable. I called on poetry to try.

THE HOME-ACHER

I wakened this morning and hovered, still covered
With blankets of lonely despair.
I longed for my bed to be warm, but instead
It was laced, all encased with cold air.

There's still the same sun, as the day has begun,
And the flowers are basking in dew,
The mountains yet reign over distant terrain,
But deep sorrow has borrowed my view.

My house has been raided, it's empty, invaded
By blue sheets of sadness, drawn tight.
What pain-powered billows; with no cushioning pillows,
Oh, "Comforter," blanket my night.

My daughter, Susie, called me quite a few years ago, when our oldest granddaughter, Kristy, at age 9, had just experienced a wonderful touch from Christ. In trying to explain it to her mother, she had said: "I don't know how to tell you this, but after I heard the message, I just felt clean all over."

I was so happy to hear this good news. I wanted to write something to Kristy that might serve to seal this in her heart, and be a sweet reminder to her of this special personal touch from God.

CLEAN

To feel **free**:
As a songbird, released from a cage,
Or a prisoner just out of jail,
Or a butterfly bursting from his cocoon,
Or a ship that's in full sail.

To feel **fresh**:
Like a chick, just hatched from an egg,
Or a baby who's just been born,
Or a toy unwrapped and not yet used,
Or clothes that have never been worn.

To feel **white**:
As the snow, as it greets the ground,
Or the cottony clouds floating by,
Or light as a fine feather's tipping touch,
Or a kite aloft in the sky.

To feel **clean**:
Like you do stepping out of the tub,
Or after a good shampoo.
It's like all of these things—yet, none of these things,
It's something entirely new.

To **know**:
He will cover the sins you discover,
His promises clearly reveal;
You are heard, you are seen, you are loved, you are clean.
It matters not how you feel.

I wrote this to my granddaughter, Kristy, who was then 13. It was just a fun piece to encourage her along the way and assure her of all the opportunities awaiting her.

AGE 13

Teenager, "green-ager",
Opening page.
Gropingly, hopingly,
Leaving the cage.

Groomingly, bloomingly,
Blossoming stage.
Dreamingly, seemingly
"Coming of age."

Lean-ager, keen-ager,
So hard to gauge,
Brightfully, rightfully
Soon to be sage.

This was written to our granddaughter, Kristy, after she was married and had begun to start a family. She had already become a most proficient seamstress, sewing absolutely beautiful clothes for her little girls. She was also conscientiously guiding them God's way and teaching them His Word. I wanted to commend her on both counts.

I framed this poem and gave it to her as a gift for her sewing room. The frame was decorated with a little sewing machine, tiny spools of thread, material swatches, rulers, buttons, zippers, needles, etc.

I must admit that it is one of my own personal favorite poems. I really enjoyed writing this one.

THE SEWING KIT

It ***seams*** we have a ***seamstress***
Of the most productive kind.
The ***material*** she uses
Was ***designed*** to ***stretch,*** to ***bind.***

She ***stitches torn*** relationships
And ***mends*** the broken heart;
She seeks ***tape*** the ***biases***
That ***tear*** the world apart.

She ***sews*** those darling ***outfits***
With their ***ruffles*** and their ***bows,***
But she also sows the wisdom
That will long outlast the ***clothes.***

Draping little bodies calls for
Clever ***alterations;***
But ***shaping*** little minds
Requires those loving affirmations.

When you ***pattern*** all their life***styles***
From the Bible, watch them grow,
As you share the way to heaven
That you ***model*** here below.

Yes, you're this special ***seamstress***
With that perfect ***fabric fit:***
For you're ***fashioning*** a child of God
With your sweet ***SOWING KIT.***

Our oldest grandson, Kevin, had always needed to sleep in the same room with our youngest grandson, Casey, because of a space problem. This was becoming more of a burden to him with every passing year. So, at age 8, when his parents finally were able to live in a larger house, he was given his very own room for the first time. When he told me about it, he was absolutely delighted. So I wrote this little ditty to him in honor of the occasion.

MY ROOM

A PLACE:

To sleep and play,
To read and pray.

To plan and scheme,
To think and dream.

For games and books,
N' cozy nooks.

For paper, stencil,
Pen and pencil.

For gadgets, favors,
Banners n' "savers".

A PLACE:

With desk and phone,
To "call" my own.

Where I can flee,
To be with "me".

To hang my clothes,
And all my woes.

For father, mother,
Sisters, brother.

Friend and guest,
AT MY REQUEST.

To shout and sing—
"My special wing"

This place—for whom?
FOR ME—-MY ROOM!

I wrote this to our granddaughter, Ashley, while she was in the midst of a traumatizing betrayal. It was to let her know that almost every person ever put on this earth will probably have a time of disillusionment, sooner or later, causing "the stars to fall from our eyes."

One of the hardest lessons we have to learn is that *life is not always fair.* But knowing this fact surely does not make experiencing it any easier.

The only One who can help us make any sense out of this life is the One who created it and us.

WHEN STARS FALL FROM OUR EYES

I'm sure, for every person born,
This fact we can surmise:
There's a day that we remember
When the stars fell from our eyes.

And, no, the world just didn't end,
The sun and moon still rise,
But life seems dark and empty
When those stars fall from our eyes.

Although the rain is hovering,
Clouds covering the skies,
We seem to just keep trying,
As the stars fall from our eyes.

And, yes, we've learned our lesson,
But what pain to theorize,
When love is at ground level,
As those stars fall from our eyes.

But, thank God, we're not helpless,
We can get up—realize,
That He can give us clearer sight
When stars fall from our eyes.

There are some experiences so painful that no person has in their possession words that might be of any help. Our youngest granddaughter, Ashley, had just been through a situation like that, which is the subject of the previous poem, as well.

These are primarily Words straight from the mouth of God, which I put into poetry form, hoping it might throw a little balm on her hurting, open wounds. I wanted her to see that God was reminding her and reassuring her that He loved her and that He had new and special plans— just waiting for her around the bend.

Little could I have guessed what sweet vindicating victories God had in store for her. After a painful divorce, she attended college, and in the spring of 2002, graduated Cum Laude, winning the award for the highest grade point average in the social studies division, an award for the best paper written in the social services division, and a prestigious writing award for best paper for the entire college. She has now been accepted for graduate school where she has been made a teaching assistant for undergraduate students.

All the way through the worst of her experiences she has remained faithful to her commitment to Jesus Christ.

TO ASHLEY, WITH LOVE

From God

I created your being, your soul I was seeing
Before you appeared on this earth.
All your days were ordained as my Book has explained,
My thoughts have been with you from birth.[1]

You know I don't sleep and my watch I will keep[2]
From your first early years, till you're old.[3]
You'll fall down, but not out; that's what I'm all about,
When "I tested, you came forth as gold."[4]

Yes, I've heard your crying, your dead-dream-denying,
But always relying on Me.[5]
So, I guarantee, just stand firm, you will see:
Deep waters will part, you'll be free.[6]

"I can's" shout anew; I have great plans for you,[7]
A future to suit your best dream.
I'll never forsake you, so no one can break you.[8]
I hold you in highest esteem.[9]

---

[1] Psalm 139:16
[2] Psalm 121:3-7
[3] Isaiah 46:4
[4] Proverbs 23:10
[5] Proverbs 3:5, 6
[6] Exodus 14:15, 16
[7] Jeremiah 29:11
[8] Hebrews 13:5, 6
[9] Isaiah 66:2b

The shattering events in our granddaughter Ashley's life precipitated an unbelievable injustice, the fallout of which also devastated our daughter and son-in-law.

The next two poems were my effort to assuage the anguish now visited upon them. The situation they found themselves in, ultimately called for a change of residence and the pursuit of a whole new direction in their lives. They relocated in a precious log cabin in a remote area of West Virginia. It was there that healing began to take place.

LOOK AHEAD

(Log-cabin-love)

They took a ride through the countryside,
And she said: "Look ahead."
Excitement grew, as they both knew
They'd found "where they'd been led."

Beyond compare, all nestled there,
A house just bound to please:
A lumbering, slumbering cabin
All logged-in amidst the trees.

At home, inside, I shared that ride,
But I saw this instead:
That perfect place, some *grace-filled-space*
Where God says: "**Look ahead.**"

It was about eight miles outside of the town of Philippi, West Virginia, that our daughter, Susie, and her husband, T.M. had resettled. As we turned in off of a paved road, the long gravel driveway to the house beckoned us to come and visit. There, nestled against a breathtaking background of huge tulip poplar trees, was their beautiful log cabin. Two sides of the house had a spacious veranda, and on it were large rocking chairs just begging one to sit and rock a spell. Our daughter's Early American furniture had made the interior into a *House Beautiful*—a showcase of country comfort. Their lot was two acres in size, and nearby was a pasture rich with grass. A herd of magnificent Black Angus cattle grazed picturesquely in the meadow. They often visited their water trough, which was situated next to our daughter's fence. Wild turkeys, deer, squirrels, rabbits and birds frequented their yard and the pastureland.

It was the perfect place for healing, renewal, meditation and writing. I composed this poem to enhance the significance of God's gentle providence.

MAYBE

Oh, God, I know you see it, all the anguish in her heart.
Won't pain and its pit-partners ever walk out and depart?
Maybe on the morrow she can borrow precious peace,
Or ***maybe,*** yet tomorrow, all the sorrow soon will cease.

Perhaps today she'll find a way to soak up lots of Son.
That rocking chair is waiting there to help her get that done:
To throw thoughts on the dung heap, all that refuse, torch and scorch,
She's lots of time to ground that grime, while sitting on her porch.

Perhaps a cow can show her how to simply graze and laze,
To swish off all those pesky (f)lies and dawdle through her days.
Perchance a deer will dart some cheer, cavorting through the field.
Like birds on wings, "all nature sings", and wants her to be healed.

I know we're promised happiness to come with morning light,
But when we are still weeping, oh how long doth seem the night.
"I can do all things through Him", the Scriptures clearly say.
This Word is true, you will come through, but ***maybe*** not today.

So, E-mail, Fax, play, read, relax,
And watch "those turkeys" run.
For, "I just don't mean ***maybe***, girl,
Your fun has just begun."

I have adored living in sunny California. We have had four separate residences there, and the last one, for ten consecutive years, was the best. It was my dream home on the top of a mountain with a view that was breathtaking. To the right we could see the Pacific Ocean and to the left we could see a part of the famed Palomar Mountain. The ranges of mountains that spread out before us was indescribably beautiful. I never planned to move. But in the summer of the year 2002 I began to realize that God was loosening me up to the possibility, a thought I did not welcome. Then came the momentous day when I received an E-mail from our daughter, Susie. It said: "Here's the deal. A beautiful house, right across the street from ours, has just been put on the market for sale. I have talked to the owners and they will wait until you get here before they make a deal with anyone." My husband was on the plane to Knoxville within twenty-four hours. He looked at the house and, after a phone consultation with me, he bought it. He arrived back in California early enough to have a realtor put our home up for sale immediately. The first persons who saw it bought it. Six weeks later we moved.

As I contemplated all that was involved in leaving my sister and some of the dearest friends I've ever had and going into a new area , the thought of starting all over again wasn't easy to face. The greatest compensation was our daughter and son-in-love living right across the street, with the added bonus of occasionally seeing all our grandchildren and great-grandchildren.

The Bible says our citizenship is in heaven. *(Philippians 3:20).* These Words have the smell of eternity on them.

MOVING WORDS

Ungrooved again, we've moved, but then
We've "done this trip" before.
We've boxed, we've sacked, we've packed, unpacked
Some thirty times or more.

But this time is most special
For our neighbors are elite;
Our daughter and our son-in-love
Live right across the street.

How faithfully He's steered as we have veered
Along life's way
To this last leg of our journey
As we head towards "sunset day."

"I know the plans I have for you,
For good," the Lord has said.
It's exciting, it's inviting,
It's such fun to "move" ahead.

Though house and climate changes,
There is one thing that's the same,
It's our "Compass" on this journey,
And Christ Jesus is His Name.

And after this He promises
Our "final move" is best.
The "location" can't be beaten,
It's that place of perfect rest.

The most ***Moving Words*** I've ever heard,
They're Jesus' Words—His Story:
"I want you with me where I am,
So you can see My glory".
(John 17:24)

As I opened this book using my son-in-law's poem to me, "The Ballad Tamer", I have chosen to end with a poem written for me by my daughter, Susie Moore.

My Mother and Grandmother died of Alzheimer's disease, which left a cloud of deep dread hovering over me. My daughter, Susie, was aware of this fact. So she wrote the following, in which she very sensitively takes my negative fear and transforms it into a positive hope.

Both her reason for writing the poem, and the poem itself, touch my heart deeply.

I FORGET

…But one thing I do…I forget.

No, I don't forget my name, my address
or my phone number. I haven't forgotten
my husband or my child.
I haven't forgotten how to cook
or how to write.
I remember how to dress myself
And how to put my best foot forward.
I can still remember dance steps
learned sixty years ago.
I haven't forgotten old jobs,
old acquaintances, old books,
old songs, old movies,
old tears.
I vividly remember walking down a road
and meeting Him
for the first time.
I remember Bible verses,
nursery rhymes,
camp songs, ant's houses
and happiness.
I will never forget my mother
playing the piano
marching my sister and me
off to bed.
The smell of perfume,
home cooking…
the crunch of snow underfoot,
the sounds of eh wind.
I have always been afraid…of forgetting.
But it seems the only things I don't remember
are…
Dearest Mom,
Thank you for not remembering all the sins of my life. All the hurts inflicted on you by those who love you most. Thank you for being like Christ. For removing from your mind my sins as far as the east is from the west. Thank you for remembering me, in love. Thank you for being the best "forgetter" I know. I love you, Susie.

"But one thing I do, forgetting those things which are behind and reaching forward to those things which are ahead, I press toward the goal for the prize of the upward call of God in Christ Jesus." (Philippians 3:13, 14)

VOICES

VOICES, VOICES,
THE WORLD'S AND *HIS*,
CHOICES, CHOICES,
THAT'S ALL THERE IS.

Printed in the United States
1494800001B/71-76